MENTAL INFLUENCE

MENTAL INFLUENCE

Magical Techniques Used to Control Other People

Draja Mickaharic

Copyright © 2002 by Draja Mickaharic.

ISBN: Softcover   1-4010-8106-1

All rights reserved. No part of this book may be reproduced or transmitted in any form or by any means, electronic or mechanical, including photocopying, recording, or by any information storage and retrieval system, without permission in writing from the copyright owner.

This book was printed in the United States of America.

To order additional copies of this book, contact:
Xlibris Corporation
1-888-795-4274
www.Xlibris.com
Orders@Xlibris.com

CONTENTS

Introduction
    Influencing Others 7
Chapter One
    Explaining the Non Physical Influences
    on Communications 9
Chapter Two
    How We Think 21
Chapter Three
    Thoughts and Mental Control 30
Chapter Four
    Perception 43
Chapter Five
    Memory 52
Chapter Six
    The Practical Means of Influencing
    Another Person at a Distance 62
Chapter Seven
    Example Suggestions for Implantation
    in the Subconscious Mind 91
Other Books By Draja Mickaharic 107

INTRODUCTION

Influencing Others

That some people may gain influence over others is an undoubted fact. This influence is usually believed to be entirely the result of physical sensory manipulation. Influence is usually applied from the influencing person to the influenced one through audible or visual stimulus. The salesman's words, the advertisers words and pictures, are probably the best and most common examples of such direct physical influence being applied by one person to influence the decisions and actions of another.

Whenever we are communicating with another person in a face-to-face situation we are always dealing with the words that they and we speak aloud to each other. However, we also both note each other's facial mannerisms and physical movements. We are aware, at least sub consciously, of what has come to be know as the body language of the person with whom we are communicating. Our noticing these physical attributes is not always a consciously directed effort on which we have focused our minds. However, the fact of our noticing these attributes, usually sub consciously has been scientifically demonstrated to be always present in any conversation through extensive psychological research. The sum of the physical sensory influences, auditory and visual, that convince us, educate us, or influence us, are only the physical or material part of the entire process of what consists of the act of communication between two people. There is also a generally unacknowledged non-physical element, which is also present in the communication between one person and another. By expanding either the physical or the non-physical element of the communication, the effectiveness of the communication between one person and another may also be expanded. Naturally, this expansion of the effect will increase the influence that one person may exert over another through the act of their mutually communicating.

That the non-physical element of the process of communicating with, and even influencing, another human being may be developed, controlled, and utilized in a practical manner, is the entire subject of this work.

Such a development of the mind of the person who desires this ability person requires dedication, persistence, and great effort. While exercises are given below to aid in this development, the exercises must be followed as they are given for the best effect in this development to take place. Desire without consistent effort brings forth little in terms of result. Following through with dedication and persistence on this work will allow the reader to ultimately gain the result desired.

CHAPTER ONE

Explaining the Non Physical Influences on Communications

The fact of these non physical influences on communications have been known all through human history, as one person had been seen to be a better communicator than another. It was early noticed that there were other influences that entered into the ability of different people to communicate, completely aside from their tone of voice, and the words they chose to speak to others with. Little real scientific research has been done on this, although most people will agree that one person is more charismatic, charming, or convincing, than another.

Among the non-scientific community, there have been any numbers of ways used to describe the variety of these non-physical processes. Most of them have been more symbolic than descriptive, but we shall examine several of these methods of description now.

Vibrations

In the latter part of the nineteenth and the twentieth century, almost all physical and nonphysical sensory phenomena were classified as vibrations, thinking then in terms either of musical vibrations, or radio waves. The metaphysicians who attempted to explain their methods of comprehending the non physical world used the term vibrations, just as those of the eighteenth century used terms of the then little understood electrical phenomena, referring to non physical phenomena in terms of charge, and positive and negative effects. In the twentieth century, workers in the field of physical sciences managed to classify audible and visual perceptions in terms of their frequencies, as measured in cycles per second, or later, in Hertz. (Hz)

Metaphysicians, occultists, and other spiritual workers jumped on this bandwagon, assuming quite incorrectly that all non-physical phenomena could also be classified in terms of frequency, waves, rays, or vibrations, as well. During the 1960's, the terms good vibes and bad vibes were used so frequently to describe non-physical 'feelings,' or intuited emotions, that it seemed to many people that this was actually an accurate statement of the true physical nature of non-physical phenomena.

However, while we may use illustrations of mental influence, while we may create analogies, give examples, and even perform experiments, with the art of mental influence, what we cannot do is accurately describe in physical terms just what this thing we call mental influence is, or how it actually operates as a physical phenomena. From a practical standpoint, it is not necessary for us to do so. Pragmatically, if it is possible for us to learn to obtain the results that we wish, we should not need to concern ourselves with the theoretical details of the manner in which these results are obtained.

Most of us have television sets in our homes. Most of us also have microwaves, and usually we own other electronic marvels, the secrets of whose operation we do not understand. If we are able to master the art of influencing other people to the degree we desire, why should it be necessary for us to have a technical understanding of the process that we are using? How many of us can actually comprehend their inner electronic workings, to say nothing of the theoretical principles of our microwave or television?

We know from both observation and experience that our mental states, and the mental states of others, are driven by our changeable individual emotional natures. It must then be obvious that until we are able to regulate and control our emotions, our minds will be completely in the power of, and under the control of, the changing emotions that we feel. We also must eventually recognize that our emotional states are the direct result of the moment. As the circumstances in our daily interaction with others changes, our emotions change and move about as well. Our emotions are as changeable as the wind, and initially they are as uncontrollable as are our constantly chattering internal thoughts.

How We Become Us

Most people believe that they live logical, rational, and orderly lives, founded on commonly accepted principles of morality and custom, that they and their neighbors willingly agree to. In fact, almost all people in any given community or society are as thoroughly programmed by the influences of their family, their society, and their community as are the computers that they use to keep track of their expenses. This is an indication that the supposedly conscious, logical, and orderly, minds of people actually have very little to do with their actions, their behaviors or even the emotions and desires that they express during the course of each day.

In fact, there are three powerful influences affecting every human being, which must both be understood and taken into consideration before the attempt is made to influence another person through magical means of any kind. The first of these powerful influences is their genetic makeup, or their biological inheritance.

Should this not be obvious, recall that a person with defective eyesight has difficulties in life that one with normal eyesight does not have. A person with physical abnormalities has stresses placed on them that the physically normal person does not have. In this sense, Biology is Destiny. Therefore, we must first consider the obvious biology of anyone whom we may wish to influence.

The second influence, of almost overwhelming importance, is the enviroment into which the child is born. This enviroment programs the child to have the experiences that mould its nature during the first dozen years of its life.

Early Childhood Training

Modern psychological science assures us that by the time a child is three years old it has gathered within itself all of the major clews and patterns concerning how it is to behave on this earth. It is these emotionally received reactions to its first three years of life that teaches the child how it is to behave in its later life. It is upon this solid foundation, of usually incorrect and always imperfect understanding, that the child begins to base all of its future emotional responses.

Modern psychological researchers have found that the first three years of a child's life are the most important to it for learning the programs that it will use to guide itself for the remainder of its life. It is during these first three years that the child's fundamental nature is formed, its basic character structure is shaped. After the third year, this fundamental programming gradually reduces in strength until about age seven. Then traumatic conditioning becomes more important; shaping the character of the child though the traumas, the child is exposed to in its daily life. These traumas, which will play a significant part in the way the child lives on the earth, are placed in the sub conscious mind of the growing youth primarily between the ages of seven and twelve, reinforcing and enhancing the earlier programming the child has received.

The stresses of puberty on the child becomes something that w\twists the growing child in a particular manner, depending on their family and cultures reaction to the process of puberty in those who pass through it. These influences may have either a beneficial or a detrimental influence upon the child, and as a result, upon the later adult. In some cases, the onset of puberty may have such a traumatic effect on the child that it later becomes impossible for them to ever become a functioning normal human being.

The third influence is the ongoing pressure of the culture and the society in which the child lives. The language the child first learns to speak always gives a special cast to its later development, as does the religious atmosphere in the home in which it is raised. The influences of others in the home, whether the child lives in a nuclear or an extended family, the influence of its siblings, contact with neighbors, and nearby relatives. All of these factors play a part in developing the child into the adult it will eventually become. The person who wishes to control the grown person this child has become must be aware of all of these many factors, and not underrate the influence of any of them.

This is why the person who going to expect to control another must be perfectly clear within himself or herself. They must be dedicated, and focused in what they are doing, and they must practice great discipline and self control.

Self Control

Thus, we must return to that ancient maxim, that one who would be in control of others must first gain control of themselves.

So far as controlling our emotions are concerned, we must first be aware that either attempting to suppress, or consciously deny any of the strong emotions that we feel will be of no avail. We must learn to harmonize ourselves with our emotions, and recognize them for what they are. Our emotions are our reaction to various situations, which we logically or illogically presume are similar in nature to other situations that we have experienced in the past. Once we can begin to observe the flow of our emotions, without being carried away by them, we have begun to grasp the handle of real emotional control.

The adult, being bound and restricted by social conventions and the desire to become economically self sufficient, moderates their emotional responses in accord with the requirements of the society in which they find themselves. Our modern psychological researchers have shown us that this necessary socially enforced restriction of our childishly acquired emotional responses, usually accomplished through their suppression, may often leads the adult into the dangerous path which occasionally leads the individual to mental illness. Far more frequently, it leads the adult into developing manageable neurosis of one kind or another.

It would initially seem that there is no rational solution to this incredible difficulty. However, modern psychologists have also found that communicating the reasons behind these unstable emotions to another, through what has been called 'talk therapy,' can often have the result of releasing the fears and difficulties that prompt them. Thus, psychotherapy, or psychological counseling, is one way of our beginning to gain control of our naturally strong emotional nature.

Understanding that one who would be in control of others must first gain control of themselves, we can next understand that no matter how we wish to influence others, our primary means of influencing the other person will be through the use of our mind. This will be true whether we are attempting to influence them through their auditory senses using words, through their visual sense as with mediums such as television or advertising, or even through non-physical means such as magic. From this, we may deduce that if we wish to gain control of others, we must next gain some control of our own mind.

The control of the mind is learned through practicing the

mental arts concerned with disciplining the mind. This is usually accomplished through mastering concentration of the mind. These arts may further may include learning to meditate, and even going so far as to learning contemplation. Once the mind can be honed into a keen instrument, the owner of the mind has the ability to use their mind as the instrument of their will, developing himself or herself further in any direction they may desire.

Developing the Mind

There are any number of mental games that can be used to assist an honest student of any age in developing the ability of their mind to become concentrated and focused. Other mental games may be utilized to develop the powers of observation, and to expand the memory. As far as training children to become mentally powerful adults is concerned, the sooner that such mental games are begun in the life of the child, the more powerful the mind of the adult will become. Like any other organ of the body, the mind will not function at its best if it is not frequently exercised, constantly expanded, and often tested.

The Doctrine of Faculties

The concept of 'mental faculties' is one that is long out of date in the world of the modern educator. However, it is a concept that is well known to the occultist, or those others who work in hidden areas dealing with the human mind. As this concept is no longer either well known by people, or much less accepted by people today, I will outline it here.

The doctrine of faculties assumes that the human mind has a number of faculties or abilities, which are quite variable in their capacity between different people. One person may have a great ability to memorize things, and thus have a great mnemonic faculty. Another may have a great mathematical faculty, which is often seen as a natural ability for doing mental calculations swiftly.

A third person may be deficient in their capacity for the memory of names and faces, but have a very well developed musical faculty.

In former centuries, it was the desire of childhood education to develop these inborn mental faculties to the greatest possible extent in each individual. Therefore, tasks were set for students, which were designed to develop one or more of these faculties. One of the more common tasks, used to develop the mnemonic faculty, was assigning a piece of prose or a short poem to be memorized every day. This piece was to be recited in school the following day. This was done to directly stimulate, increase, and thus develop, the mnemonic faculty. Today the mnemonic faculty often atrophies from the lack of such daily exercises. Children of four and upwards were expected, as late as the 1890's to recite their assigned memory piece in school each day. Naturally, as the child grew older, the content of their daily recitation piece grew both longer and more complex. In this manner the child's memory developed, and they had no difficulty expanding the amount of material that they were able to learn. The fact that this practice is actually effective may be shown by the continual use of this program in educational systems still found in other supposedly less developed parts of the world today.

Memorizing something every day is a good preliminary exercise for mental development, as it is useful even in beginning to condition the mind to the more difficult process of self-development. Short poems, selected jokes, or brief stories, are probably the best thing for the average person to begin memorizing. You should avoid memorizing anything that relates to your daily work, it is better to begin with three of four lines of light humor than it is to attempt something that might ultimately discourage you in your efforts.

Focusing Your Attention

The faculty for concentration is developed in the same manner as any other faculty, through exercise. In this case, the first step is learning to focus the faculty of attention on something outside of yourself. For many people, this is a difficult first step, as they have had no real experience with attempting to accomplish this. The majority of people today seem to be primarily focused on themselves all of their lives.

There are any number of exercises that may be used to gain the goal of focusing the attention. The most important thing is not the exercise used, but the goal of developing the attention, which is reached through the practice of this exercise. The goal is that the person should not be self-concerned, and be able focus their attention completely on something that is outside of themselves. This may be another person, or a physical object. Once the ability to focus the attention of the mind is developed, the developed focus may then be applied to anything that the person desires to focus themselves on.

Now it is possible to complicate such a simple exercise as this by insisting that certain breathing exercises are added to it, or that other, usually more complex, things are done at the same time. However, let us begin by looking at a very simple version of this attention focusing exercise. Most of us clean our own living quarters, and wash our own dishes. If we simply do our best to focus all of our attention on these mundane tasks as we accomplish them each day, we will begin to make some progress in this area.

Once you are certain that you can focus your entire attention on doing the more mundane tasks of your housework, you should then begin to focus your mind on a regularly scheduled exercise. You should also maintain the exercise of focusing your attention while doing your housework. You will be doing the housework anyway, why not gain the extra benefit of focusing your attention on the housework as you accomplish it?

One of the best exercises for focusing the mind that I know of is what I call the birthday candle exercise. To perform this exercise you will need a package of small birthday candles, the smaller the better. Sit quietly in a comfortable chair in front of a table, a kitchen table will do. Now light a small birthday candle and look at it, focusing your entire attention on the flame. Allow your physical body to relax, as you slowly breathe in and out. Without forcing your self in any way, and without any strain, concentrate your attention by focusing your mind exclusively on the birthday candle until it burns out.

In the above birthday candle exercise, your ideal is not to reach the blank minded state of the mediator; it is simply to place all of your attention on the candle flame. By directing all of your attention on the candle flame, you will find that you will be able to relax your physical body as you do this. In time, you will feel your body responding to your desire to focus your attention. Your breathing will become more regular, and your attention will waver less and less from the candle flame to other things. By maintaining the housework exercise, you will discover that you will have gained two benefits. You will become more mentally focused on doing your housework, so your work will go faster. You will also discover, often to your surprise, that your home will have somehow become cleaner.

Observation

Observation is a combination of the concentration of mental focus, and the memory. Most people have too many thoughts flowing through their mind to either concentrate on what they are doing, or to remember. They have goals and desires, emotions that dominate what they think and do. These ill thought out goals and desires, and their frustrations about not achieving them, are constantly churning around in their minds, making it impossible for them to truly concentrate their mind on what they see, or to actually remember what it was that they have seen.

Learning to focus your attention makes it possible for you to see more of the reality of the physical world, as it gradually opens your senses to what is really present. The more you are able to focus your attention on the reality of what you see, the less you will have to deal with the veils of emotion that people constantly place before themselves when they look at the world. As I have mentioned, these mental veils consist of the person's frustrated desires, and their vague, ill formed and un-filled idle dreams.

Playing Kim's Game

Once you have gained the ability to focus your attention on the birthday candle without distraction, you can begin to play Kim's game with yourself, or if possible, with a friend or two. For the best results, you should play the game with a group, or at least with another person. However, you can play the game by yourself if you have no one else with whom you can play this game.

Kim's game is the game described briefly by Rudyard Kipling in his book 'Kim.' The man who trained Kim, to assist him in developing his ability to observe and remember what he saw, used this game. The game, which makes an excellent family game, is played in the following way.

Place a number of objects on a tray, choosing a few small objects of various kinds. The tray is then covered with a napkin or a towel. Each person playing the game has a piece of paper and a pencil. The tray is placed in front of the players, and the covering towel is removed for a short time. Say for a minute. Then the towel is replaced. Now each of the people writes down each of the objects that they observed on the tray. The winner is the person who correctly writes down the largest number of objects that are actually to be found on the tray.

If you are playing Kim's game with a group, a number of trays, at least three or four, may be made up in advance. This will allow the game to move along a bit faster. Playing with a group of people who are doing the same exercises will also allow the members of the group to develop themselves faster. There is more power and a faster development that may be attained by joining into group development with certain exercises. This is one of the exercises that are useful for a group to work with.

As you become more expert in the game, the number of objects on the tray may be increased, and the time that the tray is left uncovered may be shortened. You may also improve the game by describing each object more accurately. For example, a 'green stone,' may become 'A smooth bluish green stone, roughly triangular in shape, about two inches long and a half inch high, that has dark flecks on its polished surface.'

As you gradually master these exercises, you will be amazed at how your powers of observation gradually open up. You will now be able to actually see more, and you will have gained much greater recall of what you do see. You will also find that you will be able to relax more deeply, and you will gradually discover that you no longer have a mind that is full of constant thoughts.

These exercises are very worthwhile for developing your mind; regardless of what you intend to do with your mind once it is developed. Thus, they are as good for a senior citizen as they are for a mother who wishes to train her children to have sharp minds. They are truly suited for people of all ages and conditions in life.

CHAPTER TWO

How We Think

The human brain is the physical home of the thought process. What a person may think about, as well as the manner in which they may think their thoughts, is prescribed by their culture, their education, their place in society, and most especially, by their native language. The kinds of thoughts that come to their mind at any time are based on the state of the person's current emotions. These emotions are the responses that the person has to the influences that were presented to them during their first few years of life. Naturally, this is an oversimplification of the thought process, but it does happen to be a fairly accurate one.

Psychologists and physicians tell us that the human brain is divided into three sections, each of which is the area in which certain kinds of thoughts are manifested. The process of thought itself is brought about through electrical and chemical reactions of great complexity. We know that the human brain has electrical signals transmitted inside of it. This presence of these electrical signals in the brain can be sensed and measured with electrodes placed on the scalp. Scientists use these electrical signals to diagnose mental difficulties, as well as to investigate the human thought process. We also know that scientists have also discovered that the internal chemical reactions of the human brain are quite complex.

Some scientific experimentation with those who meditate has shown that the process of meditation calms the internal tensions of the human mind. In lesser cases, these tensions are calmed almost as much as they are calmed by sleep. In the case of some experienced meditators, the individual is able to enter into a mental state that goes beyond deep sleep without apparent difficulty. When this occurs, the frequency of the electrical signals in the brain become slower, and the intensity of these signals seem, to some extent at least, to be under the control of the person who has placed their mind into that state of deep meditation. Interestingly enough, the temperature of the brain rises during periods of intense thought.

Unfortunately, no matter how deeply modern scientists have delved into the human mind, the entire process of thought is not one that has been fully understood by the investigators of science yet. Even the location of specific thought patterns and response areas in the human mind is not completely known. What has been known for centuries is that the mind is a marvelous instrument, and that it has an amazing set of abilities. Unfortunately, even with the research capacities of modern scientific investigation, we still have not learned what all of the many capabilities of the human mind may be.

Those who work in the area of the occult believe that they have some insight into these abilities. A few of these abilities are mentioned here, although this does not begin to state, much less exhaust, the list of what the human mind may accomplish.

Telepathy
The Transmission of Thought between People

In the nineteenth century, the French scientist Flammarion stated: "one mind can act at a distance upon another without the habitual medium of words or any other visible means of communication." He postulated that the signals of the mind were transmitted through the 'ether,' at that time accepted as a non-physical medium for the transmission of energy. The existence of the ether is no longer accepted by modern science. Yet, for many years many scientific researchers have generally accepted the belief that under certain circumstances, human thoughts can be transmitted from one person to another.

While there have been many accounts of the mental transmission of words, phrases, ideas, and concepts, from one mind to another, such accounts and individual experiences, no matter how important they may have been to the individuals concerned, are not suitable for satisfying the strict requirements of modern scientific research. These isolated events are not reproducible, in that it is impossible for one person to replicate what another person has done in the field. For something to be truly scientific it must be measurable, using physically sensible instruments, and the effect or effects discovered by one scientist must be reproducible by other scientists. The process of mental thought transmission, whatever it may be, seems to be neither. It obviously lies entirely in another area of inquiry or endeavor than that of the scientific.

Were it possible that we could immediately and without effort sense the thoughts and feelings of others, we would immediately know what others actually thought of us, as they would know immediately what we thought of them. The process of reading another's mind is thought to be about the same as being able to look at them, and observe what their superficial thoughts are at the present moment. If we study the varieties of experiences of this phenomenon, which have been revealed to us by many of those who have actually consciously picked up thoughts from another person, we will find that there are certain conditions which are usually, but not always, present. These most frequent conditions will allow us to further understand just what conditions may be required for the mental transfer of thoughts from one person to another.

If we examine these stories of mental thought transference, we will find that one of the most frequent linkages between the two people involved is that of emotion. Husbands often feel that they can communicate wordlessly with their wives, and wives often believe that they can communicate in this wordless manner with their husbands, as but one example of an emotional connection. The phenomena of a child mentally telling their parent that they have had an accident, or that they are in trouble, over a great distance has also been reported frequently. It is only very rarely that such experiences of mental communications have been reported to take place between people who have no emotional connection with each other at all.

Does this mean that an emotional connection is necessary for the transmission of thought from one person to another? No. It only means that in most reported narratives of such thought transmission, there seems to have been an emotional connection between the two people involved. There have also been reports of thought transmission between two people with no known reported emotional connections between them at all.

Emotional stress on the part of the person transmitting the thought also seems to play a part in thought transmission. When a person is emotionally stressed, especially when that emotional stress manifests as a need to communicate with another, there seems to be some activity that opens up within the person and allows them to send out a cry for help to the person with whom they wish to communicate. However, there have also been accounts of successful mental communications between two people that have not involved any emotional stress at all. Should this seem to be confusing to you, I can assure you that it is probably at least equally confusing to those scientists, psychologists, and parapsychologists, who have attempted to study the matter.

From the above we can see that there really seem to be no rules which we can immediately identify concerning the process of the transference of thought from one person to another.

This may be only partly true, as the description of such cases gives us the idea that emotion can facilitate the transfer of thought. Thus, we may say that emotion may increase the influence exerted by one mind on another. Where there is no emotion present, or where there is a contradictory emotion, thought transference between two people seems unlikely to take place.

Emotions and Memory

Psychologists tell us that the emotions and the memory are intimately connected within the sub conscious mind. They also state that the sub conscious mind is the strongest and most powerful part of our being. These scientists add that should the sub conscious mind oppose a decision taken by the conscious mind, it is unlikely that the conscious decision will easily be brought to fruition. Through many instances of psychological counseling, psychologists and psychiatrists have demonstrated that many of the mental ills that beset people have their roots in the fears and trapped emotional memories that are held in the sub conscious mind of the sufferer. These memories, and their associated fears, are then carried forward unknowingly into the victim's daily life.

It may be that certain kinds of fears, emotions, and memories, act to make the transmission of thoughts from one person to another possible under certain circumstances. It may also be that other fears, and emotional memories, held in the persons sub conscious mind, make it impossible for that person to be able to transmit thoughts from their mind to that of another. At present, scientists really do not know the answer to this question.

At this time, all we can say that we really do know about the subject of thought transference between people is that we do not know very much at all about it at all.

Unfortunately, those who seem to be the best at transmitting thoughts from their mind to the mind of another seem to be at the two ends of the scale of human mental stability. More unfortunately, modern science seems only to be able to study those examples that have been found at the lower end of this scale. These scientists have been able to spend a great deal of time studying those who are mentally unbalanced in some way.

Those people who are emotionally clear, mentally stable, and who have a clear and focused mentation do not seem to present themselves for psychological examination very often. Why should they? They are those people who are able to deal with the world as it is, and who are required to participate in its day-to-day affairs. They have no pressing need for psychological assistance. In fact, it is probably from the ranks of the very mentally stable that the better psychologists, psychiatrists, and psychoanalysts are drawn.

Once a person has mastered the art of focusing their mind on something outside themselves, and has learned to observe the world around them in an emotion free way, it is now possible for them to begin to monitor their own emotions. It is necessary for them to begin to see the emotions that arise within themselves, as something that is outside themselves, yet is a force that is capable of manipulating them, should they allow it. By viewing their emotions in this abstract way, it is possible for the observant person to begin to understand how, and why, these emotions have risen up from deep within themselves.

Once observation of the rapidly changing emotions has begun, it is necessary that the person observe these emotions with the aim of explaining them, and their source, to themselves. They must ally themselves with the strong emotional force within themselves, often called their inner self, so as to convince their emotions that they need not manifest in the often destructive manner in which they have been accustomed to doing in the past.

Actually doing this requires making friends with the emotional nature as if it were a very young child. Then, it is necessary to explain to the child like emotional nature that it need not be destructive in the life of the person. This takes both time and patience on the part of the learner, but this difficult task may eventually be accomplished, should the effort be sincerely made to bring harmony between the two.

Anger

Anger, one of the most destructive of the strong emotions, is usually the result of one person trying to control another person, a thing, or a situation. That the person desiring to control the other has no real right to do so is but one reason why feeling angry or displaying anger is usually not the best response to any situation that provokes this destructive emotion. Once the causes of the feelings of anger are known, increased understanding of the reasons that lie behind the emotion can eliminate them.

Anger is not only one of the most destructive emotions that a human being may feel, it is also one of the most useless in terms of making any desired changes in the behavior of another person. When there is no anger present in either party, it is often quite easy to convince another person to change their behavior. In this case, the destructive or foolish nature of the behavior must be pointed out to the offender, and the agreement of the person that this behavior is not really necessary for them to display should be obtained.

Then a better behavior in the circumstance may be suggested, and it will usually happen that the individual will conform to the suggested better behavior pattern of his or her own desire. Most people wish to 'do the right thing,' but often they do not know what the right things to do in certain circumstances are. A gentle explanation of the problem, and some words of guidance expressed without anger, is always far more effective than any emotion driven display of anger.

Frustration

Frustration is often a cause for both mental and emotional blockages. Instead of displaying emotion over the cause of the frustration, it is far better to turn away from the cause of frustration. The thoughts may then return to the cause of frustration once the emotional feeling of frustration has passed. In many cases, the emotion of frustration will make it impossible for the frustrated person to think rationally about their apparent difficulty. Naturally, this increases their level of frustration, or even adds the emotion of anger to their frustration.

When any strong emotion has captivated the mind of a person, they will be unable to rationally solve any problem they may be attempting to deal with. If the emotion of frustration is not dealt with rationally, it will usually result in the complete blockage of the person's rational faculty over the matter at hand. Of course, this often makes it completely impossible for the person to rationally solve their original problem.

Control

It is important for people to understand that they have far less control over the people and things of the world than they might desire or imagine that they have. Once the individual recognizes how little control that they actually have over the many people, things, and events, that surround them in life, they can surrender their assumed ability to control to the guidance of a higher power. The manner of doing this may be summarized in the phrase, "Let Go and Let God." Once the person is able to do this, they can begin to gradually eliminate most or all of these harmful feelings of anger and frustration from their daily lives.

The strong emotional energy generated by outbursts of emotion driven rage that overcome people due to anger, frustration, or the supposed loss of their control, become memories that tell their sub conscious mind that this is the way that they should react to similar situations in the future. Thus the tendency to display anger, rage, and frustration, builds up increasingly over the course of a lifetime, completely blocking a person's mental equipment from being truly effective.

Unless these emotions are eventually released, they may accumulate to permanently harm the reactions and responses in the daily life of the person in whom these emotions have accumulated. Learning to deal successfully with strong emotions is one of the most important tasks that are required for real growth in life.

Developing the Emotional Nature

Your emotional nature can become a sensitive instrument for judging the various physical environments and situations in which you may find yourself. Your emotional nature may also be developed to allow you to judge the true nature of the people whom you may contact in your day-to-day life. In order to become such an instrument, and for you to be able to rely on the information that such an instrument provides to you, it is first necessary for you to clear out the emotional blockages from the depths of your sub conscious mind.

There are many ways that this clearance of the emotional nature may be accomplished. Psychological counseling is one way, journal writing, or frequently speaking with your sub conscious mind; your 'Inner Self' is another. There are several other methods available, any one of which may be most suitable for you. It really does not matter which method you use to clear out any emotional blockages and lack of emotional control that you may find within yourself. What is important is that you actually take the time to do so.

Becoming clear of this emotional detritus is an important step on the road to perfecting yourself as a human being, and is absolutely necessary to becoming an effective magician.

CHAPTER THREE

Thoughts and Mental Control

Human beings usually believe that they are in full control of their thoughts. In fact, most people, especially the majority who have the least disciplined minds, have no control over their thoughts at all. They are actually the prey of their emotions, their emotion-laden memories, and of the many influences exerted on them from the various forces of the universe. In the following paragraphs, we will look at some of the many influences that impinge on people's minds and affect their thoughts.

Situational Influences

When a person works at any mundane occupation, their mind quite naturally turns to thinking about that occupation. They think quite frequently of the various problems, personal relationships, and the affairs concerned with that occupation. Were the same person working in a different occupation, or even working at a different place of business, their thoughts would naturally turn to the problems, relationships, and affairs of that other occupation, or that other location. From this we may decide that one of the major influences on the human thought process is situational. These situational thoughts deal with the details of the particular physical and social situation in which the individual finds himself or herself at the time. This is independent of whether that particular situation is occupational, domestic, or social.

Group Emotional Influences

For anyone who is working, going to school, or participating in any other group activity, such as a social event or a sporting event, it is difficult to deny that many of their conscious thoughts will deal with their current mundane activities. They have developed an emotional concern about these activities, and thus they are naturally prone to think about them. Now if there are a number of people in the group, it is only natural that the other members of this group will think about these same activities as well.

The sum total of these thoughts will influence and reinforce each other on a sub conscious level. This reinforcement of thoughts has the effect of adding to the influence that the thought process of each of those who are thinking about the subject may unconsciously feel. Thus, the more people may dwell on thoughts concerning their work, or on any other group activity, the more these thoughts will permeate their conscious mind during their presence, or even their later absence, from the situation that engendered them. Situational thoughts of this kind often make up the greatest number of thoughts with which people concern themselves during their waking day.

If those who are thinking about these things are strong willed, and if they have a good control of their emotional nature, their daily thoughts will radiate around them like a beacon. In the case of someone who has a strong mind, the presence of their strong thoughts frequently acts to draw other people into their thought processes. These strong-minded people may or may not become the leaders of the particular social group, but they often become the ones who direct the development and direction of the group, regardless of their actual social position in it. They may also unconsciously, or even consciously, set the ultimate course of the group, by influencing the group sub consciously through their thoughts.

This is a form of mental influence, although it is rarely ever consciously applied by those very few people who have the strong will and the emotional control that is necessary to accomplish this kind of subtle mental influence.

'Thought Forms'

In the nineteenth century, the members of the Theosophy Society developed a number of words and phrases to describe some of the non-physical influences on human thought. Their words are not very accurate descriptions of these influences, but they are better descriptions than the words used by many other people. Others use words that have been taken directly from the physical sciences, which they have misapplied to the non-physical realms. This misapplication of words often causes confusion in those who would study the non-physical. There are very few words in the English language that may be used to describe non-physical things. Most words that English speakers now use to describe non-physical things have been taken from other languages, such as the Semitic languages of the near east, and the Sanskrit or Hindi languages of India.

I mentioned previously that you are limited in what you can think about to the language that you use. It would seem that English is not the best language in which to write, speak, or think, about the non-physical universe. Nor does English have words that accurately describe the many things that may pertain to the non-physical universe. However, English is a language that has a long history of adopting words from other languages to describe things that are not to be found in the English language.

The word, or rather the phrase, that the theosophy society used to describe those strong willed thoughts, which a person may unconsciously project outward from themselves, is 'Thought Form.' When we are speaking face to face to someone, as at an office meeting or a cocktail party, our physical body is enmeshed in their thought forms, just as their physical body is enmeshed in our thought forms. This physical connection of the thought forms of the speaker and those of the listener is said by occultists to make communication between one person and another more complete. When another person physically enters the shared thought forms of two people, it is said that their thoughts will often be unconsciously directed to whatever the other two people are discussing.

I know of no psychological studies that have been done on this subject, and as it often happens that bringing a third person into the conversation of two other people often changes the subject, I am not certain that this idea would hold up, were it given an actual objective scientific examination. However, I believe that the idea of co-workers at a business place tending to share the same thoughts, in thinking about their business concerns, is far more accurate. Mental influence regarding the sharing of thoughts is something that is not as obvious, or apparently as common, in small groups as it is in larger groups.

In large groups, especially where there is an emotional fervor present, the sharing of thoughts between people may actually be observed. This sort of thing happens at sporting events, where the emotional enthusiasm surrounding the cheering for a favored team may cause a complete suspension of other thoughts in the minds of onlookers. The same kind of emotion is to be found at political rallies, protest demonstrations, and other similar emotion driven events. What is required is a large amount of undisciplined emotion, either favoring or opposing some cause or other. In this case, it is difficult to say if the thought form has any rational content, or if the effect found it is just the result of the pure emotion displayed. I would personally suspect that it is usually the latter.

Emotional Content of Thought Forms

The greater the emotional content of any thought form, the more liable it is to be sensed by another person. It is hard to enter a church, for example, which does not impress the solemnity and spirituality of its structure on the person entering. The older and more respected the church is, the greater this effect seems to be. As the extent of a thought form is not metrical, and thus cannot be measured with scientific measuring instruments, it is difficult to say if the emotional effect of sensing the apparent spirituality of the church is entirely due to the residue of the prayers and devotions of the believers. It may well be a product of the emotional expectations of those entering the supposedly holy place. I have noticed that on taking a blind friend with me to a church, he was struck by the apparent spirituality of the place, despite his inability to see any of the imposing architectural artifacts that I had recognized as having created that same impression in my own mind.

Environmental Influences

In addition to the influences that a person may receive from the minds of others, the situations they find themselves in, or the social environment in which they happen to be located, occultists also say that other non-physical influences act on the human mind. These influences are usually said to be, influences from spirits of the dead, influences from the planetary bodies of the solar system, and other various miscellaneous influences from the invisible world. We will briefly look at some of these supposed influences, none of which may actually be measured scientifically.

George Gurdjieff, a well-known spiritual teacher in France, who died in 1949, once said that there is a part of the human nature that is very receptive to the influences of many of the invisible forces of the universe. This part of the human nature is swayed by the planets in the heavens, the gods and deities of various cultures, and by all of the many inhabitants of the invisible worlds. Mr. Gurdjieff then added with a wry smile that this part of the human being is also very stupid.

As I mentioned, whether or not these invisible forces actually have any real influence on human beings can never be scientifically tested. These non-physical forces cannot be seen, nor can they be measured. We do know that while some people conform quite accurately to the description of those who are mentally and emotionally swayed by the supposed invisible forces external to themselves, we also know that many other people seem to be immune to any such influence from these same forces.

Human Suggestibility

The different levels of human response to the so called non-physical influences of the universe may be entirely due to the different levels in suggestibility found among various people. Suggestibility is a facet of the human nature that may be tested through psychological experiment. When a human being is suggestible, it is much easier to implant an idea in their mind. Suggestible people frequently may be convinced to believe quiet outrageous and impossible things. When a human being is completely gullible, or completely suggestible, they often may believe anything at all that is told them by another person. These two human traits are such that they are found in varying degrees in the minds of almost all people.

Often both suggestibility and gullibility come about because the particular person has no internal reference with which to compare the information that is being given to them. If they have no information, or memories, with which to compare with that which they are being told, or that which they read, they are far more likely to uncritically accept any new information that is being given them. In this case, further information concerning the subject under consideration may be of benefit in changing their minds. Through this educational process, the person may reduce their tendency to accept uncritically whatever they have been told.

Beliefs

Still another influence on the minds of human beings shapes the way that they think. This is the influence on the person of their strongly held beliefs. Any belief that has a great amount of emotion in it will have made a large and lasting impression on the person's subconscious mind. The stronger a person's belief in something is, the less likely they are to be able to change that belief, even in the face of contradictory evidence.

Excellent examples of this fixity of strong beliefs are the religious beliefs that a person learns in their early childhood. These beliefs are accepted uncritically into the mind of the child, where they become fixed and coated with the emotional overlay of every additional religious service, or other reinforcement, that the person experiences. Should the person convert to another religion, the new beliefs are layered on top of their previously accepted initial beliefs, which are only rarely, if ever, weakened or removed. This is why it is not unusual in times of stress for a person to call on the religious beliefs of their childhood, ignoring completely the newly accepted beliefs of the religion to which they may later have converted.

With these understandings in mind, we are ready to begin to consider ways of mentally influencing another person. To begin this task, we must first select someone we see reasonably frequently to influence, and we must devise a thought that we wish to implant in that person. This requires that we do some research about our subject before we begin to attempt to influence them.

Pre Accepted Beliefs

Selecting a candidate in whose mind you wish to implant a thought must also involve understanding the pre-accepted beliefs that are being held within the person. It is further necessary to accurately estimate the person's suggestibility, so that you may prejudge the effort that you will be required to make in implanting a thought in them. As with everything else, you should gather as much information as possible about your potential subject before you proceed with your work. This involves taking sufficient time to study the person whom you have selected as a test case in as much depth as it is possible for you to do so. You should learn as much about them as possible, and write down what you have discovered so that you can apply the information when you formulate your plan of approach to them. Do not trust your memory to hold all of this information for you. You will be more successful if you have written notes concerning what you have found.

Sending Thought Forms

Now if a thought, or a thought form, is to be the medium through which one person exerts mental influence on another, it must be a thought that is deliberately created, and is given a sufficient force or power by the sender to have the influence that will be required on the person who is to receive it. We might say that the thought must have a life of its own. This means that the person who wishes to send forth the thought form must take the time to deliberately create the thought form, vitalize it, and then willfully transmit that thought to the person who is to receive it.

This is the reason for the preliminary exercises of clearing the mind, and learning to focus the mind as a useful tool of the person's will. Unless the person who desires to mentally influence another has a clear and focused mind, they will be unable to create the powerful 'thought form' required to actually exert any useful mental influence on the other person. It would seem that this is not an area in which casually undertaken actions are ever likely to be successful. Only deliberate actions, undertaken with the desire to have a specific effect on a specific person, will be of any value in mentally influencing others. It is developing that powerful thought form, and applying it accurately to the specific person, that you must next consider.

Requirements for Exerting Mental Influence

Thus, we may now say that we have three important requirements for the person who would desire to exert mental influence on another:

1. They person exerting the thought must have a clear mind, free of any internal chatter, and also free of any inner emotional turbulence.
2. They person must have the ability to form a clear and decisive thought in their mind, and using the power of their will, direct that thought to the mind of the person who is to receive the thought.
3. They person must have the ability to load their focused thought with their own emotional energy, so that person who is receiving the thought may clearly receive the thought that it is desired to send them, above the background chatter of their own conscious mind.

We might also add the caveat that the thought being transmitted must be one that the person will immediately accept. It should be obvious that sending someone a thought that opposes their will, or a thought that is in conflict with either their strongly held beliefs or their real desires, should always be avoided. Understanding how thoughts operate once they enter the subject's mind is a very important point to consider in planning for thought transference.

Opposition to Receiving Thoughts

When you think of something with which you disagree totally you may feel an inner emotion of revulsion to that thought. This revulsion may cause you to put the thought out of your mind, or to turn away from the thought in some other manner. When a person receives a thought with which they totally disagree, it will not be one that will lodge comfortably within them. It will certainly not be a thought that will motivate them to action of any kind.

There have been several scientific studies done concerning the way people gain the acceptance of others. One of these may be summarized, for our purposes, by a small bit of humor.

> A man was walking down a street when he was approached by a panhandler who asked him for fifty dollars. Naturally, the man indignantly refused to give him so much money. The panhandler was not to be discouraged, so he asked the man for a dollar, which the man immediately gave him.

Most people are unwilling to make large changes in their lives or behavior. When they are asked to make large changes, the person asking them meets as much resistance as the panhandler met in his request for fifty dollars. However, should the person then be asked to make only a small change in their life or behavior, as compared to the big change they were previously asked to make, the person will usually comply. People often become willing to make the small change, to avoid making the large change they had previously been requested to make.

Should we wish to turn our subject away from something that is 'near and dear' to them, we will quickly discover that we cannot effectively do so by a direct frontal approach. If we look at the persuasive techniques used by the advertisers art we will see that we should instead hold out another attraction to the subject as a lure. By luring the subject to our viewpoint, we can point out that his former belief is a handicap to his fully participating in what we are holding out to him. He will then slowly reduced his allegiance to his former belief, as he enters into the lure we have used to bring him away.

Another way of expressing this is through the old adage; "You will catch more flies with honey than with vinegar." We must be certain that we are always armed with sufficient honey in our attempts to persuade others. To gain our honey, we must learn what motivates the person, and we must provide this motivation to them as a lure. Then we shall see them turning to us in compliance with our desires for them.

Persuasion and Salesmanship

No matter how much we may love the lure of magical practice, the simple fact is that in the art of persuasion, common salesmanship is always the first essential. The magician who has studied the psychology of persuasion and salesmanship will always do far better in their efforts than the one who has not. Verbal salesmanship is always essential a person's everyday life. Recall that wee shall be working with the subjects' mentation, their processes of thought, as well as their emotional nature.

Understanding this and other elements of the art of persuasion can give you some very worthwhile insights into just how changes in human behavior are actually made. Once you have some idea of the methodology of framing these changes in behavior, you will find it far easier to gain the compliant acceptance of any thoughts or words you may wish to send to another person. Like anything else, this subject must be studied. Fortunately there is a vast amount of material that both psychologists and salesmen have written that is available for studying in the field of influencing others, using persuasion, or salesmanship.

The art of salesmanship is an entire field of knowledge that is devoted to changing the behavior of others. Studying books about the science of persuasion and salesmanship is always a worthwhile effort for the person who wishes to influence others. There is always more to learn about motivating people to do what you wish them to do than you presently may know.

You should have prepared convincing and logical arguments to sway those with whom we are working. These arguments should allow them to rationalize, and justify to themselves, their doing just what you wish them to do. In the art of salesmanship, this is known as overcoming the objections of the customer. In some cases, this is more difficult than in others. Sometimes, at first glance, it may even seem to be impossible. Still, to influence people successfully, you must be prepared to provide rational and logical reasons that will allow the person to rationalize and eventually consciously accept, why they are doing something, often something that they might not have previously ever even in their wildest dreams considered doing.

Before we begin to attempt to influence our subject, let us consider, based on what we know of the person, just what their possible objections might be to doing what we wish for them. We then review these potential objections, and working with them one by one, think of rationalizations and justifications that the person may use to overcome each and every one of them in their mind. We must do this in the same manner that a salesman must discover reasons for the customer to purchase his product rather than any other one.

As a good salesman knows, in each and every case that it is necessary to approach the customer from the customers' point of view, rather than from the point of view of the salesman. We must constantly 'preach to the choir,' telling the subject how their doing what we wish them to do will further their own goals and desires. In this way, we will gradually get them to change their views, and eventually comply with our wishes for them.

Hypnosis, the Key to the Sub Conscious Mind

Another art that enters into gaining the compliance of others is the art of Hypnosis. Learning how to hypnotize people is a very worthwhile study for anyone who wishes to master the art of influencing others, as it is one way in which you will be able to learn just how to enter into the mind of another person, and change their behavior. Both of these arts, salesmanship and hypnosis, while they may not be not metrical scientific studies, are well worth your attention. Both of them will teach you how to change the behavior of others, as well as how to increase your own ability to get along with other people in your daily life. Later we shall have more to say about distant hypnosis, an advanced technique using a magic mirror. For now, you can consider adding the study of hypnosis to your other intellectual pursuits.

CHAPTER FOUR

Perception

We perceive the physical world through our five physical senses. Seeing, hearing touching smelling and tasting give us information concerning the physical world that we live in. Unfortunately, we have no way of perceiving the non-physical universe through these five senses, so we must learn to be content with our perceptions of the physical world in this way.

Of the physical senses, we believe that our perceptions of the world are accurate, and we believe that that they are the same perceptions as the perceptions that everyone else obtains from the same information. Unfortunately, this is just not so. Recent scientific investigation has shown that every living human being sees, hears, tastes, smells, and touches, the physical world in a slightly different way.

As an example of this, our more complete understanding of such things as the color 'Red' reveal that we have made an unspoken agreement with others to identify a certain color as being red when we see it. Thus, our belief that a color is red is actually a social agreement that we have entered into to respond with the answer red when we are asked to identify the color of something that our culture and society has identified as red. If we are going to identify a certain specific frequency of light as being red, we do so because our culture and our society identify that specific frequency of light with that term.

To go even further, the particular electro chemical changes in our eyes, and of the neural functions in our brain, that occur when we identify an object as being colored red may actually be quite different from the neural functions and electro chemical changes which occur in the eyes and brain of someone standing next to us, who also identifies the same object as being the color red. Thus, our own perception of what we may call red may not be the same as another persons perception of what they call red. Yet, we both think of what we perceive as being red because of our cultural agreement to do so.

The same apparent difficulty exists in terms of touch, hearing, taste, and smell. Only certain people may become perfume blenders, because only certain people have the delicate sense of smell that such an occupation demands. Other occupations have their own restrictions concerning the refinement of the physical senses that are required in them. Coffee and tea tasters, wine tasters, and those who make candies, all must have a refined sense of taste. Those who work in other areas must have a refined sense of sight, such as artists, whose sense of color and form must be well developed. Musicians must have a good sense of tonal pitch, as well as a well-developed sense of rhythm.

As infants, we learn what the uses of our senses require. We gradually learn the names of the various things that we will be taking for granted as adults. It is hard to remember that it was necessary for the adult to learn all of these many things as a child. Yet, a parent will take time to explain all of these things to their child, often without understanding that they are teaching the child the many social agreements that they have to make with the society in which they will live.

Now it is possible for us to intellectually understand the above few sentences without great difficulty. However, mastering the art of applying this information will take us quite a bit longer. Initially, it means that we must understand that we may never again trust anyone else's perceptions of anything to be exactly the same as our own perceptions of what we believe to be exactly the same thing.

Illusions

If you have ever seen any optical illusions, you will see another way in which perceptions can be mistaken. Another example is the 'fake' perfumes, which smell the same as name brand perfumes, to the unsophisticated senses of the average nose. These are examples of the way in which the physical senses may be tricked, or fooled into believing that something is not what it really is.

Aside from trickery that may be applied to the physical senses, the mind itself may be deceived by the way it perceives information. The information comes into the mind, but the mind perceives only what the real nature of the individuals mind allows it to perceive. Under certain conditions, the mind may perceive things that are presented to it quite incorrectly.

First:

The mind operates in such a way that we usually perceive only what we expect to perceive.

A sign I recently noticed in the office of a friend best illustrates this. The sign said, 'If you hear hoof beats think of Zebras.' He told me that he had put the sign up to encourage himself to 'think out of the box.'

Second:

Mindsets tend to form quickly, but once they have formed, they are quite resistant to change.

Once we have decided that something means something, we relax our attention, and we tend not to question that something any further. Hearing water running in the bathroom, we may decide that it is our mate taking a shower. When we see water running under the bathroom door we may investigate and discover that the sound actually was water flowing from a broken pipe. Hearing the shower water running is an expected occurrence, finding a broken pipe is an unexpected occurrence. People tend to expect the expected, the normal. They will often write something off as an expected occurrence, rather than investigate, think, or believe, that it might actually be an unexpected occurrence. This is especially true when the unexpected occurrence might be something that is either unpleasant, or unwanted.

Learning About Assumptions

While your mind will always turn first to the familiar, you must then be certain that you always take the time to question what else the occurrence might be. You not only must be willing to change your mind set, but you must actively try to avoid having a set of pre conditioned responses to any problems, or to any information that may come to your attention in your daily life.

This requires that you stop making assumptions about all of those things that you may come in contact with in your daily life. This is a very large step, and can be made only by first becoming aware of just how many assumptions you make each day. This is not an easy task, as almost all assumptions are made sub consciously. However, by gradually becoming aware of these assumptions, and then by gradually and consciously deliberately ceasing to make them, you will eventually be able to free yourself from the negative consequences of automatically making assumptions about the many daily occurrences in your life.

Third:

New information you receive on any subject will be automatically be mentally assimilated into the existing information that you already hold concerning any subject.

If you sincerely do not believe that something can be accomplished, either because you don't know how it could be done, because you have no idea why it should be done, or because you don't want it done, you will have a great deal of difficulty in actually accomplishing it.

The best remedy for this mindset is to remember the statement that NASA put on their bulletin board in their first office, when the organization was first formed. It was this:

> Anything the mind of man can conceive, man can accomplish.

That statement got NASA to put a man on the Moon, despite the overwhelming obstacles and opposition to the possible success of the venture. If you keep this phrase in mind, it will assist you in accomplishing anything that you might set out to do.

You must always bear in mind that new perceptions or information you may receive will always be added to the information that you already have in your mind. Instead of trying to fit the new information into your present beliefs, try to look at the new information as it stands alone. Attempt to see it without adding it to your present store of knowledge about the subject. Perhaps a bit of humor will make the point.

> A king once lost his throne because when his marshal came to him and told him, "Sire,—The peasants are revolting!" All the king could think to say about it was "They certainly are!" The king took no further action, and the peasants overturned his rule.

Fourth:

> The more unclear and ambiguous the information you receive is, the more difficult it becomes to clarify the information, and perceive the truth, as further new information becomes available.

When someone gives you mixed signals about something, it becomes increasingly difficult to understand where the person is actually coming from, or what they mean or want, even when they are beginning to make their true wishes more openly known. The more confused their initial signals to you, the less likely it is that you will grasp what it is that they desire when they actually begin to try and speak clearly to you. The more plainspoken the person is initially, the less confusion will be present in their interchange with you.

People who drop subtle hints about things, and expect others to understand them as serious requests, fall into this category. These people are being deliberately ambiguous in their requests, as they often have no clear idea of what it is that they want anyway. While they would like you to fulfill their vague request, they are only making it more difficult for you to do so. The initial confusion they are sowing will make it more difficult for you to comply with their request, once they are able to plainly state the request.

You might bear this in mind when you speak to others. Do not beat around the bush. Speak clearly and plainly, stating your desires. Never assume that the other person has even the faintest idea about what you are telling them, as they probably do not. You should speak clearly and in detail, telling them just what you want them to do.

Fifth:

Once any people have committed themselves to a particular

viewpoint, it becomes very difficult, if not impossible, for them to change their viewpoint.

You will find that this is especially true when you have to write a report about something. Your written report, or your public stance on any issue, becomes something that you will have great difficulty altering in time. The reason for this is the social 'peer' pressures you may feel concerning your stand, and the reaction you might have concerning the feelings of other people, should you decide to change your stance on the subject.

Lord Acton once said that the only time that you can safely change your viewpoint on an issue, once you have publicly stated your opinion, is when you seem to be put at a disadvantage in doing so. The apparent disadvantage of your new position will then gain you some public sympathy for your having changed your viewpoint.

You must bear this in mind when you are attempting to influence the publicly held position of a person. This is a case where the private view may be changed more rapidly then the public expression of that viewpoint. Like the difficulty involved in turning a large ship in heavy seas, slow and small changes in direction over a long period of time are what is needed. Do not be impatient, the change will come about.

Clear Perceptions

Forming clear perceptions concerning anything is an art in itself. The best procedure that I know for doing so is the following:

First—Write out all of your perceptions concerning the matter, based on all of the information that you have available to you at the time.

Second—Make note, on another sheet of paper of what you would expect from the matter, and what your personal desires are for the matter. Note your inner emotional responses as you write this out, as they will reveal to you your real desires in the matter. You may find that they may be quite different from your originally perceived desires, or your beliefs about the matter.

Third—Going back to the first sheet, eliminate all of the information on the first sheet that you find on the second sheet. The information being eliminated has obviously been shaded, both by your expectations, and by your personal desires.

Fourth—On a third sheet of paper, make a list of all of the assumptions you have made concerning the case. Grade this list in terms of their probable accuracy, one being the most accurate, and the highest number present being the least accurate.

Fifth—Compare these assumptions with the information you have available to you. How much of your information results from inaccurate or unreliable assumptions? Use this as a sieve to sift out the remaining facts.

Sixth—Once you have done this, re write the remaining information on another sheet of paper. This is what remains.

Seventh—Taking the remaining information, look at it from a new perspective. How much of it fits into your desires or goals in the matter? Based on this information, is what you wish to obtain even possible for you to obtain? If you find that it is not, you had best abandon the matter rather than waste further time on it.

Eighth—If new information comes in, write it out on another sheet of paper, and then pass it through the same process, adding it to the final information sheet only if it passes though all of the above tests.

Once you have clarified your perceptions of the matter you are able to look at the matter and begin to make rational decisions concerning it. If you have a friend whom you can consult with concerning this matter, ask them to review the final sheet and give you their opinion. Remember that new eyes often see more clearly than old.

NOTE:

Some of the information in this chapter was abbreviated and adapted from chapter two of the book *'The Psychology of Intelligence Analysis'* published by the Center for the Study of Intelligence of the United States Central Intelligence Agency at Washington D.C. in 1999. I recommend this book to those interested in learning to think clearly.

CHAPTER FIVE

Memory

Our memory is what makes learning possible for us as human beings on this earth. Psychologists have identified several components of our human memory, and have assigned various names to them. We all have sensory information storage, a short-term memory, and a long-term memory. When I spoke of the mnemonic faculty previously, I was referring to the long-term memory. The distinctions between these three types of memory, and some explanation of each of them, are given below.

Sensory Information storage and short term memory are beset by severe limitations of capacity, while long term memory, for all practical purposes, has a virtually infinite capacity. It is this virtually infinite capacity of an individuals long-term memory that we shall make use of in attempting to influence others mentally. In our efforts to influence others, we shall be attempting to place information into the subjects' long-term memory. We shall be working with this implanted information to influence our subject.

Our sensory information storage receives sensory impressions from the five physical senses. It holds this information only long enough to allow the brain to interpret what it has received. It is due to the short-term nature of this memory that we are unable to recall the physical feelings of pain and suffering that we might have felt in the past. That these feelings may be recalled under hypnosis is a sign that the memories have not really left us, but also that the memory of these experiences is one that is inaccessible to our conscious mind.

Our short-term memory receives information from our brain that has been processed from the sensory information storage part of our memory. The short-term memory holds this information for further processing, and then sends it on to our long-term memory. There are severe limitations on the capacity of the short-term memory, and as a result, it can quickly become overloaded, should we attempt to remember to many things at one time. The number of things that can be retained in the short-term memory is determined physiologically for each person. Unfortunately, there is no known means of training the short-term memory to expand its capacity.

Our long-term memory receives information from our short-term memory. It accepts uncritically the information and impressions that our short-term memory gives to it. When the short-term memory is overloaded, the information sent to the long-term memory may be severely restricted by time limitations. Information is stored in the long-term memory by a very complex electro chemical process, and through forming connections between brain cells known as neurons.

I am certain that you have noticed that if you sit quietly in a relaxed state, your brain will begin sending up random thoughts to your conscious mind. These random thoughts are known as brain chatter or 'The chatter of a thousand monkeys,' as one well-known spiritual teacher has put it. Brain chatter is caused by the presence of unresolved emotional energy in these supposedly random memories, or often in other memories, to which these supposedly random memories are connected in some way.

All of the memories stored in your long term memory are stored in a huge network that is all connected together, much as a spider web is made of an inter connected patch work of single strands. Thus, all of these memories are connected together in what any outside observer would consider a random and crazy quilt patchwork. Your memory has the capacity to contain a full lifetime of thoughts and experiences. The problem people have with their long-term memory is not ever its capacity. The problem always lies in their being able to access the proper memories, at the proper time.

The retrievability of your memories is influenced by the number of locations in which information is stored, and the number and strength of the pathways from this information to other concepts that might be activated by similar, or apparently similar, incoming information. The more frequently a pathway is followed, the stronger that path becomes, and the more readily available is the information that is located along that pathway.

Reverie Exercise

One of the great mental exercises, which should be done with a timer to facilitate its proper development, is to sit in reverie, and trace the first random thought that comes up in your mind back to its source. Follow all of the associated thoughts in turn, and see how the first random thought is connected to many, many, others deep within the depths of your mind. This should be done for no more than five minutes at a time for the first week or two of daily practice. Ultimately, this exercise may be expanded to ten minutes each day. However, doing this exercise for a longer time each day is not recommended without close guidance by a teacher.

The second exercise of this nature is to select one item in your memory, or any desired idea you might wish, and tracing the thought of it back slowly through your mind, making a mental or audible note of all of the interconnections, and the other memories and thoughts that this item is connected to. This exercise should be done with a timer as well. You may use a tape recorder to speak keywords, which may be used to trace the pathways audibly, should you desire to do so.

The second exercise should not be started until you have practiced the former exercise for ten minutes a day for at least two weeks. There are reasons for giving the exercises in this way, and practicing them differently will not give you the benefit from them that you will ultimately gain if you do them correctly, and in the proper order.

Memory and Learning

There is obviously a great connection between memory and learning. After all, learning is essentially a process of connecting a number of bits of information together in the memory. When information does not fit into what people know, or into what they think that they know, the person has great difficulty in processing the information. When the information is something that people already believe that they know, their memory will first accept that part of the information that is most in agreement with what they believe that they know. In some cases, this easy acceptance of some information can act to keep out of the memory information that conflicts with what the individual thinks that they already know. Unfortunately, this selective acceptance of new information frequently acts to keep the person from actually learning anything new.

It is for these reasons that it is important to look at every new bit of information you receive without assuming that you have any knowledge of the subject at all. Learning not to make assumptions about anything is a very important part of learning how to learn. Mastering the art of making no assumptions is difficult, but it can be accomplished. When you work on developing your memory by tracing out random thoughts, you will find that you must approach this without making any assumptions at all of what you may find.

Otherwise, you will find yourself mentally following down pathways that will be based entirely on your assumptions and expectations. This practice will ultimately lead you nowhere at all.

Processing Information

Psychologists have shown that the greater amount of processing that is required to store information in your memory, the more likely it is that you will remember the information, and be able to access it when desired. Thus, if you wish to remember something, it might be of assistance to connect this memory to something of a similar nature that you have learned in the past. One way to do this is by making up a story about the new information, creating a mnemonic aid, or connecting the information to other information in some other way.

For example, to remember the name of Putin, the current (August 2002) president of Russia, you might recall that he was *Put In* office by the former president.

This is why people say that in being introduced to someone you should repeat their name, and then speak the name in a sentence of some kind. 'Mr. **Smith**, I am pleased to meet you. I know that **Smith** is a common name, but I really have only known two **Smiths** in my life. You sir, are the third Mr. **Smith** I have met." By speaking slowly and distinctly, as you normally would under these circumstances, you are generating a connection with the person's name. This is something that will encourage the name to go into your long-term memory and remain there.

Another suggestion that has a similar beneficial effect, which you might wish to use when meeting a person, is to look at the person's eyes and memorize the color of their eyes. When you do this, you are directly and deliberately paying attention to the person. This will assist you in remembering the person, and it will give them material non-physical-assistance in forming a more favorable impression of you.

When the information you must remember is of a more complex nature, you may wish to make up a story about it, or connect it with something that you already know. For example, there is a silly ditty concerning the various brands of beer that are on sale at a local campus tavern. The ditty weaves the names of the various beers into a very brief story. The ditty has no literary merit at all, but memorizing the ditty allows all of those who serve beer at the tavern to remember the names of the various beers that the tavern has available.

'Learning the ropes' is a phrase that is now applied to learning any new job or position. It was originally applied to the art of learning the various ropes used to hoist and trim the many sails on a sailing ship. These ropes all were attached to the tariff rail of the ship, on the main deck, by the use of belaying pins. One of the things that you are attempting to do in reading this book is to 'learn the ropes' of your own mind.

What you need to do is to locate the various belaying pins you may need to anchor new facts into your mind. Your long-term memory is the tariff rail of the main deck of the ship of your mind. From that point, ropes reach up as far as the maintop sail, or into the furthest recesses of your memory. You need to know which belaying pin it is that anchors which rope, so that you can hoist, trim, or furl the sail of memory you wish to work with, whenever it becomes necessary for you to do so.

Using a mnemonic device has great merit, as you can add new information to the memory aid as you wish. Once you can recall the mnemonic device, the information you desire is at hand. A typical memory device is the word HOMES, which refers to the names of the five great lakes, Huron, Ontario, Michigan, Erie, and Superior. There are undoubtedly already several mnemonic devices that you already know and use. Do not be afraid to add more of them, you will find that they are all quite useful to you.

The better able you are to organize your memories and experience in your long term memory, the better recall you will have of the facts and information that you will require in your daily life. Naturally, this will improve your work performance, and this of itself will make your life a bit easier. A good memory, with good recall, is one of the greatest assets that a person can have. There is no reason that you should not develop one for yourself.

The Working Memory

Your working memory is that part of your long term memory that allows you to keep track of the information you are currently working on in your mind. Many years ago, it was discovered, through psychological research, that the average person could keep seven items in their working memory, plus or minus two items. This means that people may keep between five and nine items in their working memory at any one time, but their working memory will hold no more. It is this limitation on the number of items in the working memory that make it difficult for some people to stay focused.

If you are concerned about something, that concern immediately becomes an item in your memory. (1)

If you are emotionally wrought up about something else, that becomes another item in your working memory. (2)

Now when something happens in the household, or at work, that throws another limitation on the number of items you can keep in your memory. (3)

If you are listening to the radio while you are working, that limits your memory as well. (4)

With four items already in your working memory, soon your mind, or at least your working memory, is completely full. Then you may say to yourself, quite truthfully, 'I can't think!'

Working Within the Limitations of the Working Memory

The best way to utilize this natural limitation of the working memory is to externalize information. Write down notes, facts, and any other things you may wish to use to solve the problem on which you are working. Then organize these facts and rewrite them in an orderly and organized manner. Now you have found a way in which you can break down any problem into its component parts. By working with the various parts separately, you will be able to reduce the complexity of any problem you may wish to solve considerably.

It always pays to simplify any apparent problems you must deal with. Once the problem is broken into its various structures, the problem is usually not so overwhelming. In fact, the original problem has usually become a number of much lesser problems. These smaller problems are certainly always much easier to solve, once they have been broken into their component parts.

Please remember, no problem is un-solvable. Any problem that you can think of may be solved, even though it may be impossible to actually utilize the solution that you have found to the problem at the present time.

The amount of attention and emotion that is focused on a memory influences not only how it is stored, but also its retrievability. Memories associated with traumatic emotional events may be placed into the deep sub conscious, where they are out of reach of the ordinary mental recall of the conscious mind. Memories that you focused your full attention on at the time, as well as memories of experiences that were pleasurable to you, are often charged with positive emotions. Frequently these pleasant memories are quite easy to recall.

The same will be true in the mind of any subject that you may wish to influence. The only difference is that you have made a conscious effort to rid yourself of these emotion-laden memories, and they have not. You will find that you will be able to use the emotion laden memories of your subject to your advantage, by attaching the ideas and information you wish them to adsorb to the memories that they already have placed deep inside themselves. To do this you must realize that all people have both pleasant and unpleasant memories. You will wish to attach the information you wish your subject to have to their pleasant memories. Fixing it in such a way that they will connect the information you wish them to adsorb, to the pleasant memories of some of the more pleasurable experiences in their life.

Emotion in Memories

All memories are stored with at least some emotion in them. The greater the charge of emotion in the memory, the more likely it is that these memories will influence the person's life. This is why recalling these memories, both pleasant and unpleasant, and discharging the emotion from them, is a necessity in clearing your mind. Until you have almost no emotion in any of your stored memories you will be attached to them in such as way as to cause them to continue to act on your life.

The process of ridding yourself of these memories is one that you will not find difficult once you begin to undertake it. As any emotion laden memories come up into your mind during the course of this work, you must take the time to rid yourself of them, by explaining the memory to yourself, and then releasing any emotion that is in them. You will continue to free yourself of these memories all your life, there is no reason to stop doing this while you are learning something new.

Focus

When you are mentally focused on something, your working memory is dealing only with the item on which you are working. At the same time, your short-term memory is processing only the information you are giving it. This is the optimum condition for studying, or for learning any new subject, as your mentation is entirely directed, and single pointed focused toward the material you are working on.

Combining this directed mental focus with taking notes, making a diagrammatic model of your thoughts, or externalizing your working memory by writing, means that you will be operating at maximum efficiency toward the goal of learning the art of mental influence. Naturally, this same process may be used to learn any other subject.

Being Disturbed

Many people who attempt to learn the art of influencing others only get so far in their efforts to master the art. This is not because they cannot master the subject. These people usually stop because they find things inside themselves, when they are clearing out their own minds that are upsetting to them. You cannot really control others unless you are clear yourself. Therefore clearing your own mind always becomes your first priority, no matter what you discover about yourself.

No matter what you find inside yourself, you must just allow it to be there. These disturbing memories will be there anyway. Once you remove all of the emotional energy from these disturbing memories, they will no longer have any effect your life. This is what leads to a clear mind. You are seeking that goal anyway.

CHAPTER SIX

The Practical Means of Influencing Another Person at a Distance

There are several magical techniques for mentally influencing people without their knowledge. Once you have learned everything you can about the person whom you are to influence, you must select the specific technique that you wish to use. This depends on how difficult you believe it to be to change their mind or influence them, and how important their compliance with your desires is to you. Aside from the less complex candle burning spells and similar things, there are three major techniques used to influence people magically. These are, Emotive Visualization, Hypnosis While Asleep, and Distance Working. We shall look at each of these techniques in turn.

When your goal is to have the person change their emotions toward you, especially if it is your desire to have them fall in love with you, *Emotive Visualization* is probably the best technique for you to use. In this case, whether the person is asleep or not when you do the work on them seems to be relatively unimportant.

When your goal is having the person change their mind about you, or changing their view about some subject that is dear to you, you are seeking a mental change. Either *Hypnosis while Asleep* or *Distance Working* are usually the best techniques to use in these cases. For success in applying these techniques, the subject of your work must be asleep. Obviously, this is more necessary in Hypnosis When Asleep than it is in Distance Working. We shall now investigate these techniques at some depth.

Emotive Visualization

If you can remember the first time you fell in love, you will have an idea of what emotive visualization is about. In this technique, you sit quietly and in a physically relaxed manner, and with your focused mind, you visualize yourself caressing and kissing the naked body of your subject. You can feel their skin under your hands, you can feel their lips on yours, and you will soon feel your tongues interact. As your hands explore the body of your subject, you will soon feel their physical arousal. Then your exploring hands confirm it to you.

Your desire in this visualization is to erotically stimulate, or sexually arouse, the other person, whom we shall refer to as your subject. The actual effect of this mental work is being transmitted to the subject as you are visualizing it. However, it will always take time for this impression to make its way from the sub conscious mind of the subject to their conscious mind. Only over the course of time, as your subject is able to rationalize and justify their changing emotions concerning you, will they be able to admit the changed emotions of love, which they will be beginning to feel for you, into their conscious mind. Until these impressions reach their conscious mind in an acceptable form, they will be unable to respond to them. You should do nothing that would identify you as the source of the emotions the subject is feeling. In time, they will make the 'first move' towards you.

Then your response should be one of cautious interest, not over eager demand.

As with any other magical technique, practice is necessary to bring the work to perfection. As your skill level in visualization of the erotic scene with the subject improves, your successes will come much faster, and be of better quality. This occurs because your influence becomes stronger, and more direct. Your projection will change from gossamer hints of warm emotion to overwhelming blasts of emotional lust as your abilities continue to improve.

When you begin using these simple mental techniques, you must expect that it will take from three or four weeks to several months, before you will see any results from your work. The exact amount of time will depend on how well trained your mind is, and how detailed and perfect your visualization of the scene with your subject becomes. Be patient, this technique has proven itself over hundreds of years. It is in use today among many primitive tribes.

You should dedicate two twenty-minute sessions each day to caressing and petting the nude body of your subject. Keep notes of each session, and review them once each week. Observe if you sense the subject replying to your caresses, or initiating stimulation of their own. The first time you work with this technique you should select a subject that you see often, but one you have never displayed any erotic interest in. Work with them twice daily for three months, and observe their changing attitudes toward you. By the time that three months has past, you should be receiving some very positive feedback from the subject.

An additional useful exercise in conjunction with this is to see yourself in a pleasant social situation with the subject. My personal favorite is walking with them in a park on a spring day. I visualize myself walking with them holding hands, both of us radiating that charm known as 'being in love.' As I ride the bus to work each day, I visualize this scene with my current subject on the (usually) ten-minuet bus ride. Of course, I do the same thing on the return ride in the afternoon. It is certainly a better use of my time than reading the advertisements.

Between these two techniques, it is possible to have anyone become romantically interested in you, regardless of their initial attraction to you, or lack of it. What is even more interesting is that this technique, once it is mastered, may be used in other circumstances as well. Of course, if you are looking for a business arrangement your visualization will have to be different than if you are looking for a romantic connection.

If your desire is to make the person favor you, you should visualize a situation that is favorable to both of you. In this situation, there is a mutual sharing of joy and pleasure, or a connection or communion present between the two of you. You might begin by seeing yourself acting harmoniously with the subject in this situation, and then feel the other person's emotion of joy and happiness at being placed in this situation with you. The overwhelming emotion they should feel, and that you should be projecting to them, is one of deep pleasure and happiness that the two of you are sharing this experience

One example of using emotive visualization in a business context might be your visualizing that you come to the subject, having achieved a large and favorable contract for something, which will benefit them in some nebulous way. You visualize yourself telling the subject of this, and feel your mutual joy and pleasure at having won the contract. The two of you share your pleasure and celebrate the award of the contract together, feeling comfortable and happy with each other because of this shared pleasant experience.

Emotive visualization works because of the repetition of the emotional scene you are mentally and emotionally projecting toward your subject. By projecting this scene toward them twice a day over the course of several months, your subject will gradually begin to overcome their natural resistance. As they overcome their natural resistance, whether it is great or little, they will gradually begin to turn themselves to you in the manner that you wish them to do so.

This follows the slow and gradual way that all of these distant mental influences methods operate. The mental and emotional pressure is sent out to the subject from the operator, and over time, the operator gradually overcomes the initial resistance in the targets' sub conscious mind. This is something that may only be accomplished by persistent effort on the part of the operator. This persistent effort allows the subject to rationalize and justify their changing relationship to the operator, which they must explain to themselves. Once they have completely rationalized and justified their sub conscious thoughts, they will gradually begin to manifest these thoughts consciously. This eventually results in the conscious physical manifestation of the operators desires for the subject, what ever they may be.

Emotive visualization may be used in conjunction with either of the other two mental influencing techniques. In some cases, as when a very large change in the subject's behavior is desired, using both emotive visualization, and one of the other techniques will make this change more possible to accomplish.

Hypnosis while Asleep

Hypnosis while asleep is accomplished using a magic mirror. Naturally, the person using this technique must first be able to use a magic mirror successfully. This is a natural prerequisite to using this technique, as is some experience in the art of hypnosis. Both Hypnosis while Asleep and the following technique, distance working, are quite effective. In most cases, they are equally effective, although some people quite naturally prefer one to the other. In any case, the particular technique being used depends on what the operator prefers, and what they believe the individual subject might be most receptive to.

In some cases, the technique to be used is determined through divination, although it may also be determined depending on the nature of the influence that the operator wishes to cast on the subject.

The Technique of Hypnosis while Asleep

In this technique, the subject is implanted with suggestions when they are asleep. Sleep is the deepest hypnotic state possible, as their is no recollection whatever of hypnosis being practiced on the individual when they awaken. The amnesia of hypnosleep cannot ever be completely removed. Further deep hypnosis treatment may reveal that the subject has been hypnotized, but the details of any suggestions that have been implanted within the subject will not ever be revealed.

In the technique of absent hypnosis that we are using, the subject is first called into the mirror, and it is ascertained that they are actually asleep. If the subject is sleeping, the operator now counts the breaths of the subject. They should be breathing at the rate of six or seven breaths per minute. If they are breathing faster, wait until the subject is more soundly asleep.

The purpose of working with a sleeping subject is to bypass their critical faculty, without awakening them. Therefore, the hypnotic approach must be very gentle, and the hypnotist must speak in a soft but confident voice. Once the operator has verified that the subject is sleeping, and has observed them in the mirror for a while, while counting their respirations to six or seen a minute, the operator proceeds as follows.

"This is (authority figure, such as 'Your Guardian Angel,' 'St. George,' etc. This must be suited to the subject, and decided on in advance.) speaking. You can hear my voice but you will not wake up. You can hear my voice, but you will not wake up."

Because the subject is in a deep sleep, this statement should be repeated several times over a minute or two before it penetrates the subjects sub conscious mind. The repetition of this statement must be made using the same soft but commanding voice over the course of at least two minutes. Once the message penetrates into the sub conscious mind of the subject, there is usually a flicker of some kind on the face of the sleeping subject. The operator should watch for this flicker in the mirror. Until there is some clear indication of the subject having received the message, the operator should continue with the same phrase:

> You can hear me, but you won't wake up.
> You can hear me, but you won't wake up.

Under no circumstances should the operator say 'You can her me but you can't wake up,' as the use of this phrase will induce panic in some people who have a fear of death. It often causes them to immediately awaken, usually with the sound of a voice ringing in their head. While most people will interpret this as a bad dream, there will now be defenses formed against further working with this person using either hypnosis while asleep or distance working. The operator should stick with the given phrase,

> You can hear me, but you won't wake up.

If a clearer signal is desired, the operator can ask that the subject provide one. However, it is better if the operator become used to reading the automatic flash signal from the sub conscious mind of the subject that will show briefly in the mirror.

> You can hear me, but you won't wake up.
> You can hear me, but you won't wake up.
> You can hear me, but you won't wake up.

I will know that you are hearing my voice when you move your index finger (lick your lips—or some other sign). I will know that you are hearing me when your index finger moves. You can hear me, but you won't wake up. You can hear me, but you won't wake up.

The instructions calling for the sign to be given should be repeated at least twice over about two minutes time. When the sign from the subject is received, this communication opening may be halted. The suggestions to be implanted may now be brought out. Obviously, these suggestions should have been well thought out in advance, and written down for the reference of the operator. Relying on the memory is relying on a frail tool when work of this kind is undertaken. The operator must continue to speak softly but with authority, and in a gentle but commanding voice.

The operator must obtain the subject's agreements with each suggestion, and when any blockages to implementing the suggestion have been removed. Whenever possible, all blockages to implementing any of the suggestions given to the subject must be removed. If there are obstacles to the subjects agreement with any suggestion, which cannot be completely removed, it is possible to tell the subject to ignore any suggestion that it seems they will not accept.

"I see that you do not wish to accept that suggestion. You may just ignore that suggestion for now. Pay no further attention to it, and ignore it for now."

When you have finished giving the subject the detailed suggestions you have prepared for them, your final task is to remove the hypnotic state and return the subject to the natural sleeping state. This is accomplished by telling the subject that they will sleep soundly throughout the night, and awaken in the morning feeling perfectly refreshed and relaxed, with no memory of this conversation.

Hypnosis while asleep produces good results, but in most cases, more than one session is required to obtain the best implantation of the desired suggestions into the mind of the subject. As with all other methods of mental influence, the operator must be patient, and have a well thought out plan of action before beginning.

Introduction to Distance Working
To Mental Influence Someone
by Distance Working

Distance working is the process of directly and consciously mentally influencing another human being, without their conscious knowledge. It is a means of gaining influence and a degree of control over another living human being. All who are successful in any form of business or profession uses conscious influence over others, at least to some extent. Concealed conscious influence over others is one of the keystones of the magical art, and as such is the goal of almost all magical practice.

That distant influence can be exerted on others has been researched occasionally by those involved with psychological research of the nature of dreams and dreaming, as well as by parapsychologists. The work of Drs. Stanley Krippner and Montague Ullman of the dream laboratory at Mamonides Medical Center, Brooklyn New York is an example of the scientific research that has been done in this field. These investigators found that the dreams of a sleeper could be influenced, in their own words, telepathically. During 74 experimental sessions, the dreams of the dreamer were influenced in 52 sessions to a point that the researchers considered significant. In only 22 sessions were misses recorded. This research was cited in 'Beyond Mind,' by Mons; published by Samuel Weiser, Inc. in 1985. Dr. Stanley Kripner wrote a report of the phenomena in 'Advances in Parapsychological Research of Psychokinesis' published in 1977 by Palanum Press, NY. Dr. Montague Ullman wrote a report of the experiment in 'Dream Telepathy', published by Turnstone in London in 1973. This and similar psychological research can be considered to be the scientific foundation of the magical practice of distance working, should such a scientific foundation be required. Obviously, the occult practice of this art takes this to a much further extent than just influencing the dreams of the subject.

In the nineteenth century the French scientist Flammarion made note that "one mind can act at a distance upon another, without the habitual medium of words or any other visible means of communication." In 1816, Dr. Arndt hypnotized a patient of his over a distance of twenty miles. Dr. Barth did the same, hypnotizing his wife at a distance of several miles. These experimenters found that a person in the comatose, sleeping, or physically relaxed state, could be subjected to hypnotic influence over a great distance. However, when the person was awake and distracted, as in eating or dancing, the hypnotic influence exerted on them had little or no effect. The same results are to be found in the magical practice of distance working. The fact that the magical practice of distance working can be taken much further than influencing the dreams of a chosen subject will probably eventually be investigated in psychological laboratories, and then reported by scientific investigators as a new discovery.

That distance working can be done which will produce lasting and beneficial practical effects in the life of the person being influenced has been long known to magicians, quite probably for thousands of years. As a magical technique it has a great deal of promise for the magician who wishes to use it to heal physical or mental conditions in others, or who wishes to favorably influence the day to day behavior patterns of those with whom he works.

While real behavioral changes may be made in practically every person worked with through this means of hidden influence, it must be recognized that distance working is always a very time consuming process. It is a means of influencing others that always requires a deep dedication to their task by the magician. Many magicians will find this technique onerous for the simple changes of daily behavior that are often desired in the actions of a particular individual. In this case, the use of a less time consuming magical technique is usually indicated.

While many magicians seek the ultimate 'easy' method of exerting influence on others, it soon becomes obvious that distant influence is not the 'easy' method being avidly sought. Distance working is a technique that, when properly applied, can yield astounding results. When it is not applied over a sufficiently long period of time, or when it is not applied with sufficient frequency, it will usually be found to result in few if any changes in the behavior of the subject.

In the worst case, the person who is being influenced will only rarely realize that there has been any effort directed at influencing them at all. It is this lack of the recognition by the subject of any external influences being applied to them that is one of the greatest advantages to be found with the technique of distance working.

The Technique of Distance Working

The Prerequisites

The following text has been written for the practicing magician. This means that the reader is assumed to have a trained mind, as previously discussed, with the ability to concentrate their thoughts. There are other assumptions made concerning the reader as well, one of which is that they have perfected themselves in one of the many schools of magical practice, and that distance working is simply another technique, which they will add to their already established list of magical abilities.

Unfortunately, this text is entirely valueless for those who cannot properly use the information given in it. The reader who is not a practicing magician is best advised to become one before going any further into the study of distance working.

Before you begin to study distance working, it would also be beneficial for you to obtain a good practical working knowledge of the theory and practice of hypnosis. Hypnosis is a subject that is of value to the average magician in their daily life and practice. Yet, I have never seen it mentioned as having any direct value to the practicing magician in any of the magical texts I have read. The real benefit of the study and practice of hypnosis is that it allows the magician to experience directly just how the human mind operates at the level of the subconscious. The magician may apply the knowledge of the human sub conscious mind gained from his study of hypnosis to his daily work, increasing his ability to guide those who come to him into paths that are more suited to their successful behavior.

There has been a great deal of information published recently in the textbooks and journals of psychology and physiology. With this valuable information available to anyone with a library card, it behooves every magician to make themselves familiar with the scientific literature and apply their increasing knowledge of the fields of psychology and physiology to their work on a daily basis.

It has been said before that magicians are natural psychologists. As with the natural artist, there are always greater benefits to be obtained by filling out a natural talent with academic training, than are to be obtained by relying only on native ability. Few artists of note have avoided having to train their natural talent by disciplined study in their chosen field. Magicians should strive to increase their effectiveness by training themselves in elementary psychology.

Personally, I consider the mastery of hypnosis and a solid acquaintanceship with the present state of the art of psychology to be the keystones of successful distance working. If you are serious about mastering distance working as a magical technique, I strongly suggest that you first master hypnosis. The perfection of the art of distance working lies in understanding just what happens within the human subconscious mind. It is this part of the mind which distance working seeks to influence, just as it is influenced in the processes of hypnosis, or even through the actions of modern consultative or clinical psychology or psychotherapy.

Another way in which the act of influence at a distance may be viewed is through the art of salesmanship. When you seek to influence another human being you are seeking to sell them something. In distance working, having your subject accept and act upon the ideas and information you present to them, your sales presentation if you will, is you goal. It is only natural that you find that the person, whom you are trying to influence, will have some objections to changing their behavior in the direction you desire.

Through overcoming the objections of the subject you will 'make the sale,' making changes in their behavior according to your instructions. The difference between distance working and selling an idea or a behavioral change to a person consciously, is that the person who is the subject of distance working will give the magician their real objections to making a change in their behavior. The subject will supply the subconscious root causes of their otherwise rationally verbalized objections. The subconscious mind of a subject will be free with information, which the conscious mind would normally suppress. Overcoming the objections of the subconscious mind guarantees that the subject will accept your instructions.

This procedure is very much the same as is done in hypnosis. The hypnotist deals directly with the subconscious mind, to rid the subject of whatever has been a barrier to their functioning adequately in their daily life. The hypnotist then instructs the subject in the behavior that they wish them to follow in the future, by implanting suggestions in their sub-conscious mind. In the case of the psychotherapist, or the hypnotherapist, there is conscious recognition and acceptance by the subject of the healing work that has been accomplished. The subject has consciously given the therapist or hypnotist the ability to influence them, to improve their behavior in some way.

Once you have mastered the practical aspects of hypnosis, and can hypnotize a subject of average suggestibility, you are ready to learn the art and practice of distance working with subjects of your choosing. The selection of your first few subjects for distance working is important, as you must select from among those whom you know and see personally on a frequent basis. This is necessary so that you can observe the results of your work on them as it proceeds. By observing the changes in those whom you see frequently, you will gain the confidence you require to ultimately be successful with those people whom you do not see very often, if you see them at all.

Initially you should limit yourself to those friends and acquaintances of which you already possess good clear photographs. These photographs will provide you with the focus that you will initially require. You must be able to see the results of your work on your subjects as it proceeds, so that your confidence in the results of distance working increases and becomes firm. While most magicians have some understanding that distance working, like many other magical techniques, can be accomplished, it is always best to watch the results of your efforts develop before your eyes. This increases your self-confidence, and makes the work much easier for you over time.

Understanding how distance working operates, and gaining personal confidence in its many beneficial effects, is greatly enhanced through following this simple procedure.

THE FIRST LESSON

To begin the learning process, the first act of distance working will be one of freeing a person from whatever negativity may be surrounding them. This is a passive means of distance working, but it is a technique that often produces astonishing results. There are a number of ways in which the minor spiritual cleansing of a person at a distance may be accomplished. We shall select a passive technique with which to begin our work, a technique that will often show strong positive results in the subject's daily life.

Select from your photograph album a picture that you have taken, preferably a Polaroid, of a person whom you see frequently. If you have photographs of two or three people whom you see daily, or almost daily, these are ideal. Now for the next three days, whenever you meet any of these people, examine their astral nature. Select the individual from this group whom you believe currently has the 'dirtiest' aura.

This person will become your first subject. To start the distance working cleansings with this person you must place a small dish in an inconspicuous place in your home, and every evening for the next two or three nights, place the photograph of the person in the dish, with the picture side up. You must then place a fresh egg over the photograph. Pray, over both the egg and photograph, that any negative influence surrounding the person be drawn into the egg. Leave the egg and the photograph in place overnight. In the morning cast the egg into the toilet, breaking it, and flushing it away. The following day, look again at the person's astral nature and you will note that the negativity surrounding them has decreased. You will often see a daily decrease in the negativity surrounding the person as you continue to perform this work with them.

Regardless of how negative the person, or the circumstances in which they find themselves, you will find that after three nights of distance working treatment with the egg there will always be a noticeable clearing away of the astral negativity surrounding them. You may continue this process with any given person as long as you wish. You will find that it will have remarkable benefits in keeping the individual clear of even the worst forms of either external, or self-generated, negativity.

Once you have witnessed this demonstration of change in the aura surrounding a person due to the simple technique of distance working, you will begin to accept that distance working can generate the strong effects that are claimed for it. You may now set out eggs for each of the persons whom you have selected as subjects. For those you see daily, place eggs over their photograph each evening, about an hour or so before your bedtime, removing and disposing of the eggs each morning before you go to work. On the other hand, there is no real reason why you cannot have the eggs on the photographs all day long.

You will now probably begin to notice that there are different 'speeds' in which any individual responds to the cleansing of their astral nature. For some, the cleansing of the aura can be completed with one egg. Others will require a greater effort; say placing eggs on their photograph every night for a week or more.

You should purchase a Polaroid camera, if you do not have one, and begin to accumulate a series of photographs of those with whom you associate. It is not usually difficult to obtain photographs of your friends and associates. You should do so as quietly as possible, and without arousing suspicion as to the purpose of the photographs. Ideally, these should be single photographs. Pictures of each of the individuals alone, posed against a plain and uncluttered background give the best effect. Group photographs should be avoided, as it is more difficult to work with them.

If you share an office or workplace with three or four other people you can begin to raise the level of stability and calm in your working environment by cleaning the auras of your co-workers on a regular basis. This will usually have a beneficial effect on your own astral environment, as there will be less negativity for you to contend with at your workplace. Photographs of your co-workers and fresh eggs are all that are required to accomplish this.

Before we go on to the more time consuming processes of formal ritual distance working, we shall cover a few other simple distance working techniques through which the human aura may be cleaned of accumulated detritus at a distance. We will begin by listing the egg technique we have been using, along with some others, so that we will gain a better understanding of how these distance working cleansings operate.

EGG CLEANSING

Egg cleansing is used to remove negative energy and negative influences from a person. It is effective in the removal of emotional difficulties caused by self-inflicted negativity or those caused by minor external influences. While it will not prevent a person continuing a negative thought train, it can be used to make self-inflicted negativity less damaging to the person. Used on a daily basis for a month or so, it often makes it almost impossible for the average person to maintain their original negative thought patterning.

Place a photograph of the person who is to be cleansed on a plate or a dish. The dish is required to catch the inner content of the egg, should it break while over the photograph. Pray over an egg that it adsorb the negative energies surrounding the subject, whose photograph is under it, and place the egg over the photograph of the person. Leave the egg in place at least an hour, preferably overnight, or even for a full day in extreme cases. Several eggs may be used, changing them every day.

The Prayer made over the egg should be something like the following, although any desired variety of sincere prayer might be used.

I pray to Almighty God the creator and sustainer of the universe that this egg remove all negative influences surrounding _____ N. _ N._____, whose photograph is displayed here.

Variations and Comments

According to some workers, duck eggs are said to be preferred to chicken eggs, I have found little or no difference in their action. Chicken eggs are obviously much easier to obtain.

It may not be obvious to the novice, but a whole fresh egg must be used. A hard-boiled egg will have no effect whatever. Under no circumstances should the egg be deliberately broken over the photograph.

If the egg should break or crack over the photograph of its own accord, it is an indication of an unusual amount of energy around the subject. This energy can be either positive or negative, and no judgment can be made as to the nature of the energy from the egg's breaking. The egg residue should be discarded; the photograph rinsed clean, under cold running water, and allowed to dry completely. Another egg should be placed over the dried photograph as soon as possible.

This is not a sign that the person is under psychic attack. It is only a sign that there is an excess of energy surrounding the person. In most cases, it is negative energy, which really needs to be removed. This is usually an indication that the egg cleansing should be continued with the subject for at least a full week, quite possibly even for a month or longer.

Eggs rarely break unless the subject is under extreme emotional stress or tension. In these cases, the person should be monitored frequently to observe the effect of the distance working cleansing.

If it is at all possible, the person should receive a thorough spiritual cleansing, followed by a blessing.

ABSENT WATER CLEANSING

Absent water cleansing, or distant water cleansing, is used to remove general negative astral influences from a subject. It is temporarily effective in the removal of minor emotional difficulties, but it will not prevent a person from calling these emotional upsets back to themselves. It is very useful to insure a good nights sleep for a person who has been traumatized by some upsetting emotional experience during the day. The magician can use this technique upon himself should he so wish.

Take a glass of water and a photograph of the person who is to be cleansed. Pray something similar to the following over the water:

> "This is the water of exorcism that will remove malefic influences from _____N._N.____, through the medium of their photograph."

Place the photograph face down over the glass of water and leave it for at least an hour. The glass and photograph should be left like this overnight, if it is at all possible for you to do so.

When the water has adsorbed sufficient negativity, empty the glass using the anti-dexter hand, and rinse out the glass three times.

Variations

If there are spirit influences surrounding the person, small bits of cocoa butter should be placed on the water. These adsorb energy from the spirit and sink to the bottom of the glass, or may they even turn black and sink to the bottom of the glass.

To dissipate negative influences from a person, and free them from negative emotionalism, place a small amount of camphor on the surface of the water. A piece the size of a match head will do as well as anything larger. As the camphor dissipates into the air, it will drive off the negative influences surrounding the person.

Herbal teas that adsorb specific influences may be used in place of ordinary tap water. In this case, the tea should be allowed to cool to room temperature, or below, before it is placed in the glass, and the photograph placed over it. It should be unnecessary to remind a trained magician that hot water will not accept nearly as much of the non-physical energy of a prayer as cold water will.

FLOWER CLEANSING

This technique might be called a distant astral cleansing of the subject. It can be used to clear away the astral detritus from a person, but as is the case with most spiritual cleansings, the action is only temporary. The technique is simplicity itself, and may be used before a person is expected to arrive for a visit, to insure that they have come to the magician's home without any particular negative influences surrounding them.

Brush the photograph of the person carefully but completely with a flower. A white carnation is usually used, but a white rose or a chrysanthemum will also have a very positive effect. The photograph can be brushed from top to bottom to eliminate the astral detritus surrounding the person.

I have heard that by brushing the photograph from bottom to top with a white rose the person will find their path to spiritual growth more easily opened. In my own experience, I have not noticed any particular difference in the direction of the brushing manifesting in the aura of the individual, but this may be my own subjective perception.

To have a person accept the instructions of a distance working session more easily, brush the photograph with a marigold blossom, while praying over it that they accept the information and instructions which you are about to impart to them.

THE SECOND LESSON

The Ritual Practice Of Distance Working

Introduction

There are five distinct steps to the ritual for distance working. Each of the steps is important, and each step must be followed in order. These steps can be summed up as follows.

1—Candles
2—Summoning
3—Working
4—Dismissing
5—Candles

1—The Candles—

The purpose of lighting two candles, one on each side of the magician, in the ritual of distance working is both to afford light for the operation of distance working, and to protect the magician from the subject striking out at them while the magician is working with them. The candles, by the form and stability of their flame, will indicate the directed astral currents, which may be surrounding the barrier, formed between them and the trace of the subject upon which the magician is concentrating.

Generally, the candles are lit, first the left and then right. In a culture in which the language is written from right to left they are lit in that manner, from right to left. This would seem to be more a function of the belief structure of the culture than anything else.

By observing the candles as the magician works, he will have continuous evidence of the astral influences, which the subject is sending to him, in return for the work he is doing upon them. Only the most naive will believe that a subject will ever express gratitude to them for any healing or other positive work done on them.

2—The Summoning—

The summoning is the calling to the magician of that part of the person with which the magician desires to work. The part of the person is called from the person to the place where the work is to be accomplished by the magician. Summoning is a separate field of magical training, and it is assumed than anyone who is interested in learning distance working is already sufficiently practiced in the summoning of both spirits and the various parts of the living human being, to make any further instructions in this area superfluous.

It is generally recommended that summoning be done with a trace, a photograph, or better, a simulacrum. This last is considered the best trace that may be used. As in other cases of summoning, a trace need not be present if it is not available.

Despite some opinion to the contrary it is quite possible to summon a person, a spirit, or parts of a person, when neither the name, or any trace, is available. This type of summoning can be done either through the assistance of a friendly and co-operative spirit, or through the technique of forceful summoning where the magician demands the presence of a particular spirit, or a non-physical part of a living human being.

While it is always easier to summon a person when the person being summoned is comatose or sleeping, that is not necessary either. The most important part of the summoning is that it be accomplished in a correct and clear manner. The magician must clearly know what it is that they are summoning. They must address that part of the subject they are calling to themselves. Once the magician has summoned that part of the person they desire to work with, they must work with that part of the person exclusively until they release it by dismissal.

3—Working

The most important part of the distance working process is actually working with the subject. The work session must be carefully prepared for in advance of the actual ritual. The magician should have previously prepared at least an outline to guide him through the exact procedure that he intends follow. This requires the magician first set out in writing a detailed statement of just what it is that he wishes to accomplish with the particular subject, both in terms of short-term goals, and in terms of long-term goals.

The following outline will be found to be helpful in most cases.

1—Determine what changes the person should make in their life. This is the goal of the work. Next, you must determine if the subject really wants to make changes in their life. Where the subject does not want to make changes in their life, the magician must write out questions for the subject's subconscious mind. He must do this so that he may learn why the subject does not desire to make the supposedly desired change. The answers the subject provides to these questions will form the basis for the subjects 'objections' to the magicians 'sale.' The magician must overcome these objections in the subject.

The magician then scans the future and learns what effect the proposed changes in the life of the subject will have on them in the future. The magician must find beneficial reasons for the proposed changes which he is encouraging the subject to make. These beneficial changes must be ones that will manifest consciously within the subject in the near future, say within the next six months.

The magician must verify, through the subject, how long it will take these favorable changes to manifest in their life. The information which the magician gains in this way becomes the 'benefit' which the subject will reap from 'buying' the magicians instruction and direction, or 'making the purchase.'

Lastly, the magician must query the subject's subconscious mind, asking, "If you were going to change your life in this direction, what would you have to do?" The answers, from the subjects subconscious mind, will provide the magician with the information he will need to guide the subject to make the desired changes in their life.

If the person's egoic nature manifests, either through the process of questioning them, or when working with them, the magician must point out to the subject's subconscious mind that it is their egoic nature that is destroying them, and limiting their life. He must show that their egoic nature is acting constantly against their best long-range interests. The magician must always encourage the subject to limit and control their ego. At the very least, the magician must expose the egoic nature to the subject so that they can see just how destructive it is to the eternal parts of their being.

The magician must always attempt to work through the egoic nature to get to the real person behind the ego. One way in which this may be done is to summon the subconscious mind of the person into the trace, and then summon the egoic nature to reveal its true self into a small magic mirror. The two are then confronted with each other, while the magician points out to the subconscious mind that it is the egoic nature, that it sees before it, which has been destroying its otherwise good prospects in life. The magician may then ask the sub conscious mind if it is now willing to cease paying attention to the egoic nature, which it can now see that it can master.

The magician should then spend several sessions assisting the subjects' subconscious mind to master the subjects' egoic nature before going on to other work. It may be necessary to make the confrontation several times, but the result, even in the case of a very strong egoic nature, is always worthwhile.

Once the magician has gathered the required information, he must write out his notes and prepare the detailed arguments he will use when he speaks with the subject. The magician can make up a set of instructions for the subject in the form of an affirmation if desired. This is often the best way to start when initially working with a subject.

An example outline might read:

> Subject: Leo Change: Reduce smoking to improve health.
> Effect: Easier breathing and lose current chronic cough.
> Time Allowed: Six months.

An example affirmation that might be used in the above case could be: You are not a person who enjoys smoking. You recognize this, and are reducing the number of times a day you smoke. You find each time that you smoke your distaste for smoking grows. You will soon be able to smoke only once or twice a day.

Further information on working with subjects is given later on in this material. Example affirmations and statements are provided, as well as complete details on the ritual part of distance working. All of this information must be understood and mastered before an attempt is made to actually practice the occult process of distance working.

4—Dismissing

The process of dismissing that part of the incarnate human being with whom the magician has worked is as important as the ceremonial dismissal of a summoned spirit from a magic circle. The importance of the formal dismissal is for the same reason, and to the same purpose as the required dismissal of a summoned spirit from the circle. It is a step that can never be ignored or slighted. In distance working, dismissal always requires that the magician who has been working with them bless the part of the incarnate human being that has been worked with. This blessing must always be given at the dismissal. If a blessing is given for any reason during the process of the working session, dismissal must follow immediately.

It is not necessary that the blessing at dismissal be long, sonorous or exotic. All that is necessary is that the departing entity be blessed as it is dismissed. A typical blessing at dismissal that could be used is:

"Depart now and return to complete (the subject) __N.__N.__, and may the Lord God Bless you and keep you, now, and forever." (Amen)

5—Candles

The candles should show, in the way they burn, stability of form of the kind which is expected before the summoning, after the dismissal. This stability must be established before the candles are extinguished. It should not be necessary to point this out, but as with other candles used for magical, religious or spiritual purposes the candles should be snuffed out with a candle snuffer rather than pinched out or blown out.

LESSON THREE

**Ritual Procedure for Distance Working
With the Sub-Conscious Mind Of a Subject**

This same procedure is used for working with any other part of the subject's being. The only difference in the procedure is the part of the person being summoned, and the manner of working with the person. Generally, working with the subconscious mind of the subject is the most productive. When other parts of the subject are worked with, the major differences are in the way the magician relates to these parts of the subject, and in the information he requests from them, or gives them.

It is always best to begin by working with the subconscious mind of a subject before working with any other part of their being. Experience working with the sub conscious mind of a subject prepares the magician well to allow them to work with other parts of the persons being.

Arrange a comfortable workplace on a desk or a table. A comfortable chair should be provided for the magician to sit in, as the procedure may take a few hours. The two candles should be about a foot or more apart, and about a foot and a half from the front edge of the desk or table. This allows space for the papers and the work outline, which the magician must have at hand to refer to as he works. A notebook and pen are also useful in making notes of the working session. The trace should be centered behind the candles.

If no trace is available, a magic mirror can be used to good effect. The magician should now relax and prepare himself for the working session ahead, which may be, and often is, both long and tiring.

Light the candles, allow the flames to attain stability, and then summon the sub conscious mind of the subject through the trace, by name, or as desired. Open communication with the subconscious mind of the subject with the following statement:

> "You have within you things that trouble you. These things trouble you because they contain unresolved energy. The unresolved energy causes you excessive discomfort and irritation. Energy is contained within these things because they are unresolved emotions. I would like to help you understand these things, so that you will be able to release the energy in them, and as a result, be happier. Once the excessive emotional energy is released, you will be happier. You will feel lighter and more carefree, because the excessive energy in these emotions weighs you down. When you have released the energy in these emotions, you will do your work better. When you have released the energy in these emotions you will have a happier life."
>
> "Do you trust me to help you understand these things so that you can release this excess energy?"

The answer of the subject is either YES or NO.

If the answer is YES, proceed with the work. If the answer is NO, there is a question of ethics as to whether or not to proceed. If the subconscious mind of the subject does not trust the person doing the work, it would probably do no good to proceed. If there is no immediate answer, the magician must pause for a short time and then repeat the entire statement from the beginning. In no event should the magician show any impatience, or any desire to speed up the process of communicating with the subconscious mind of the subject.

Once the agreement of the subject has been obtained, the following opening may be made. This opening should be used regardless of how tentative the agreement of the subject may have been when it was given.

"We will develop our friendly relationship slowly. We will begin our friendship by working with small things first. To develop our friendly relationship you must select the difficulties that you want to have me help you resolve. Now it is your turn. Give me an example of something which you would like me to assist you to understand."

The subjects' subconscious mind will present something that it perceives to be a problem. The magician must explain, and de-energize the apparent problem. Once this is accomplished, the magician asks the subject: "Is there any reason why you should not release all of the energy from this problem?"

If the subconscious mind answers NO, the magician instructs it to release all of the energy from the problem. Once the energy is gone, either the magician should sense the change in the subconscious mind of the subject, or the subconscious mind of the subject should inform the magician.

If the subconscious mind of the subject cannot release all of the energy within the problem, the magician must again work through the difficulty, assisting the subconscious mind to prepare to release all of the energy within it. Again, the subconscious mind is told to release the energy, and again more energy is released. This must be done until there is no more energy remaining in that particular problem.

The question above is asked again: "Is there any reason why you should not release all of the energy from this problem?" The same procedure is followed until all of the energy in that problem has been released.

Once all of the energy has been released from any one problem, the subconscious mind should be instructed to present another problem that can be resolved. The new problem should be worked with as discussed above, until all of the energy has been released from it. The magician may now tentatively propose something that is in accordance with the instructions he intends to give the subject.

"Would you like to tell me why you desire to smoke?"

If the subconscious mind of the subject follows this up, it will present situations around or concerning its smoking habit. The magician can eliminate energy from these situations until there are no further barriers within the subconscious mind of the subject to the instructions of the magician.

This entire process will usually take several sessions before the subject is clear enough to be able to accept commands or instructions from the magician. It is not unusual for a magician to take a month working every night with a particular subject before they are clear enough to accept positive commands from the magician into their daily life. The process of clearing away the internal blockages of the subconscious mind is the most difficult part of distance working. Unfortunately, it is also the most important part.

Once the subconscious mind of the subject has discovered that it can have blocked emotional energy released through the agency of the magician, it will usually become enthusiastic about the process. Any subconscious mind has a vested interest in releasing blocked emotional energy. At this point, the subconscious mind of the subject becomes allied to the magician. The magician should take advantage of this fact to have the subconscious mind begin to bring up those memories and beliefs that are within his field of interest for the subject.

"Now bring up to me those reasons why you feel that you should smoke, so that we can examine them together."

"Now bring up to me those experiences that have convinced you that smoking is an enjoyable experience, so that we can review them, and decide together if the memories of these experiences are correct."

Once these areas have been investigated, and any energy contained within them released, it becomes much easier for the magician to command the subject to reduce their smoking in a way that will make them comfortable with their reduction of the habit patterns and nicotine addiction.

This is the reason why first reducing the internal stresses of the sub conscious mind is so important in those cases where the subject has an ingrained belief, or a patterning, that would oppose the direction in which the magician wishes to take them to improve their life. Until these sub conscious stresses have been released, or at least greatly modified, there is an internal barrier to the subjects accepting the positive instruction that the magician wishes to implant within them.

This same process has its counterpart in hypnosis. Reading the literature of hypnotherapy before beginning this process will make the work easier and more understandable for the magician. It is my personal belief that distance working is more effective than hypnotherapy, as the subject, being unaware of it, can place no barriers to it's effect within their conscious or sub conscious minds.

CHAPTER SEVEN

Example Suggestions for Implantation in the Subconscious Mind

I would like to thank my former student Mark Thallenger for these excellent example suggestions.

The type and form of suggestions that can be successfully implanted into the subconscious mind of a subject follow generally those suggestions that are used in the art and science of hypnosis. In distance working, as in hypnotherapy, it is possible to first remove all of the barriers to the implantation of any specific suggestion. While this is entirely possible in hypnosis, and is infrequently accomplished in hypnotic psychotherapy, it is not usually a feature of the average hypnotic procedure.

When suggestions are made in distance working, they must be made in the same positive manner, as commands, rather than as the weaker suggestions often found in hypnotic suggestion or in recited affirmations. Weak and tentative suggestions, those that the subconscious mind has the ability to ignore, defray, or defer, will have no permanent effect upon the lifestyle of the subject.

Instructions that conflict with the root beliefs of the subject must be held to a minimum. One of these suggestions given over a six-month period is sufficient to begin with. The effect of each of these suggestions must be noted. In the case of changing the root beliefs of a subject, it usually requires that the magician remove the more negative energy and the limiting beliefs of the subject before the subject can proceed to act upon the suggestions that they are being given.

Whenever possible the subject must be physically observed frequently, to ascertain whether or not they are actually incorporating the implanted suggestions into their lifestyle. It will be found that most subjects can incorporate only one suggestion into their lifestyle every six months or so. The magician must arrange his goals for the subject accordingly, so that he does not overload the subject with suggestions that they will find difficult, or even impossible, to successfully implement.

With these caveats, the following suggestions have been found to be suitable for the specific difficulties indicated. They may be used as desired, and as indicated in the case of any particular subject.

Female Breast Development

One of the first impetuses to learning to master distance working came from a young woman I was dating at the time who was painfully conscious of her very small breasts. One day she said to me that since I was a magician I should be able to do something to correct her breast size. I asked her if she would like me to attempt to do so, and she said that she would. I then hypnotized her and gave her the suggestion below. That night, I began reinforcing the suggestion using the distance working technique, as explained in this material. I then made it a practice to hypnotize her twice every week, and work on her at least five nights a week with the distance working technique as well. Within six months, her breasts went from a 'slight A' to a full 'B' cup. Success had been obtained!

The suggestion I used in both hypnosis and in distance working was:

"Your breasts are a symbol of your ability to nurture and give of yourself to others. As you increase your ability and desire to nurture and give of yourself to others, you will find that your breasts will grow in size and become more attractive. As you desire your breasts to be firmer and more attractive, you will find that becoming more nurturing and giving will not be difficult for you. Your desire to have attractive breasts will insure your becoming more nurturing and giving of yourself. You will become more nurturing and giving, and this will be reflected in your increasingly attractive breasts."

"Within the next few days this process will begin to take place. You will know that it is happening because you will feel a slight tingling in your breasts. You will find some reason to comment on it to me (or to ___ N. ___). In that way we will both confirm to ourselves that you are becoming more nurturing and giving of yourself, and that your breasts are developing as you desire."

Physical Comfort

I have found that even in the coldest weather some women in New York City insist in wearing the absolute bare minimum of clothing. While this is quite attractive in a heated building, this can make trips to and from cabs, to say nothing of subway rides, uncomfortable. Faced with these circumstances one of the young ladies I was seeing challenged me to keep her warm with magic. I used the following suggestion in working with her using the distance working technique, selfishly adding that she would always be warm and comfortable whenever she was in my company. After a week's work on my part, our Saturday night date on a chilly November night was successfully enhanced by her not being overly cold. It took me three more weeks' work to insure that she was both warm and comfortable on all of our dates. Any emotional energy that has programmed the person to think that they must be cold must be removed to accomplish this. The human body warms itself by increasing the metabolism, so there may be a tendency for the person to eat more in cold weather because of this work.

"You are always physically comfortable and completely at ease no matter where you are, no matter what the temperature is, no matter how you are dressed. You never feel too hot, you never feel too cold. You automatically compensate your body heat for changes in the surrounding temperature. You automatically compensate for changes in your body temperature caused by your dress. You will now find that you are always physically comfortable, and at ease, regardless of your dress, or your surroundings."

Hate

Hate is one of the most destructive human emotions. Having to work closely with a person who was consistently hateful and negative about everything in their life, I began working in them with this suggestion and the distance working technique. It took me six months to discharge enough of their negative energy to get the person to be reasonably neutral to things. While most of the people in the office believed that the person had a real change of character, I knew better. I had another six months work to get rid of all to the negative hate energy that they had inside them. This accomplished, they were at least satisfactory for me to work with. This work was completed without the person concerned being consciously aware of it at all.

"You have found that the hate you direct toward others always falls back on you. This directed hate has caused you much pain and suffering in the past. You know that you must cease hating if you are to have a successful life. You desire to have a successful life, so you will no longer direct hate or negativity toward ___ N. ___, or toward any one else. You will now find that you no longer have the strong emotion of hate present within you."

Happiness

The same man, now less hateful, but always bitter, was the recipient of the following suggestion after I had cleared out his hate. Within another year, he became actually fairly pleasant to work with.

"You have found that what you think makes you happy is not what really makes you happy. You have discovered that true happiness comes from within. You desire to live a happy life, so you will now become increasingly happy as time goes on. You will find that the happier you are, the happier those around you are. Your internal happiness will soon become apparent to all who meet you, so that within six months you will be thought of by all who know you as a very happy, and completely satisfied person."

Attention—

A professional hypnotherapist of my acquaintance gave the following two suggestions to me. He suggested that I use one of them on the young lady whose breast size had been increased, as he thought that she was too much of a 'clinger.' Unfortunately, we broke up before I began using the suggestions on her. However, I see no reason why these suggestions should not work in situations where they might be required.

"You have discovered that you are not the center of the universe. You have discovered that you do not require constant attention from others. In the future, you will require decreasing amounts of attention. Within six months, you will discover that you really require very little attention at all. This discovery will please you, as you will now be able to give yourself all of the attention that you require."

ALT: "You will discover that all of your primary attention needs are fully satisfied by an occasional smile from ___ N. ___. This discovery pleases you very much, it makes you quite happy and satisfied."

Destiny

This is another suggestion given me my by Hypnotherapist friend.

"You have discovered what kind of a person you are. You know what it is your destiny to accomplish and become in this life. You know that this destiny may best be accomplished by __(make pre written suggestion here)__. You have made a decision to accomplish your destiny and have a fulfilling life. You realize that nothing can stand in the way of your decision to fulfill the destiny that you were born to attain. From this day forward you will do everything that is required to accomplish your destiny. You will turn away from everything that would lead you away from fulfilling your destiny."

Inhibitions Fears

This suggestion is very useful for those who suffer from irrational fears and phobias. I have used it successfully on several people to rid them of this kind of fears.

"You know that you have had within you irrational and unreal beliefs. These irrational and unreal beliefs have caused you much pain in the course of your life. You have now rid yourself of these irrational and unreal beliefs. From now on, you will avoid acting on these irrational and unreal beliefs. You now realize that they have no value to you. You now realize that there is nothing in the world that you need to fear."

Relationships Clarification

This is another suggestion from my Hypnotherapist friend. He and I discussed this problem and he used the suggestion on me during a time when I was confused about my relationship with a girlfriend. It worked for me.

"You know everything about yourself from the moment you were born. You have the ability to develop a complete harmony between your subconscious and conscious minds. Once you are in complete harmony within yourself you will better be able to act on the world outside yourself."

"Within your sub conscious mind is all of the information you need to clarify your relationship with _____ N. _ N. _____. During the next few weeks, you will consciously clarify your relationship with _____ N. _ N. _____. After __(date)__ you will find that you are able to understand your relationship with _____ N. N. _____ completely. This will assist you in bringing about a more complete harmony between your conscious and sub conscious minds."

Relationships Affection Problems

This suggestion was used to successfully stabilize a marriage that seemed to be on the rocks.

"You know that you have a deep and abiding love for __N. _ N. __. All of your efforts must now be concentrated in consciously accepting just how much you really care for and love __N. _ N. __. There is no reason why you should not completely consciously accept just how much you care for and love __N. _ N.__. You admit to yourself that __N. _ N.__ is the only really special person in your heart, and that you truly love them. You know that __N. _ N.__ is the only person whose opinion is important to you, and that you really love them with all your heart. You will soon be able to consciously tell them how much you really love them."

Relationships Separations

When I moved away from New York City for three years, to go for some advanced professional training, my girlfriend at the time and I separated. When I returned, she was still not seeing anyone else, and so we began dating again. This suggestion, used by myself as an affirmation, made it easier for me to resume the relationship.

You know that you were happy while you were in contact

with __N. N.__. You know that you are not happy with your life as it is now. You remember that the time you spent in contact with _ N. N. _ was the happiest time of your life. You must return to _ N. N. _ so that you can be happy again. You know that you will never again find the warmth and affection that you found when you were in contact With _ N. N.__. You know that the time you spent in contact with _ N. N. _ was the best time of your life. You know that you will never receive the kind of care you received when you were with __N. N.__."

"You will (find a way to) return To _ N. N.__, so that you can have a happy life again."

Listening And Paying Attention

This suggestion was used on a person who worked in my office. They never seemed to know what was going on, and were as out of touch with the world as could be. I discussed the problem with my hypnotherapist friend, and we came up with this suggestion, which I used on the subject for three months. At the end of the three months, the person was a better listener, and much more in touch with what was happening in the world around him.

"You are a person who must think before you speak. You realize in the past that you have offended others with your speech. In the future, you will be able to understand just what you must say, and how you must say it to avoid offending others. You will no longer offend others with your speech, and this will make you happy and content. In your daily life, you will use simple language, so that those who hear them understand your words. When you speak to others, you will project the feeling that you are a warm, sincere, and caring person. Others respond to you in this way. You speak to others in a way that insures that they will respond favorably to you. You listen completely to what others have to say to you, and you respond to what they say. You will now find that people give you more respect because you listen to them, and you give them direct attention when they speak.

Over the next few weeks, you will realize that your ability to communicate successfully with others has increased greatly. This will make you very happy. You will now understand that you may now suit your reply both to the words that people consciously speak and to their sub conscious motivation without judging either.

General Difficulties

"Whenever `A' occurs you will have feelings of `X'. You will think of `X' and remember not to `A'. (Or, remember to avoid `A')
As an example of the use of the above is:
'Whenever you have a desire to smoke you will remember that you are not a person who enjoys smoking. You will think of this, and the thought will remind you that you really do not want to smoke."

Basic Outline for Working with the Subconscious Mind of a Subject Once Favorable Communications Have Been Established with the Magician

A. Produce the Argument

The argument should be written out in positive statements. The statements of the argument must imply a decision by authority with which the subconscious mind must agree. The argument must be the set of instructions that it is desired that the individual accept into their subconscious mind and make a part of their life.

B. Locate the Blockages

This must always be accomplished with a positive statement. Bring us a habit, belief or memory that keeps you from doing (acting) in the way you know that you should.

C. Resolve the Blockages

Using the rational faculty of the magicians conscious mind.

You have presented to me a belief that _____. I will now explain it to you, and show you why it will not prevent you from _____ as you know you should (or must).

D. Obtain the agreement of the subconscious mind that it can accept your explanation.

I have explained to you why the (habit, belief, memory) of ___ that you presented to me will (must) not prevent you from ___. You have learned that this (habit, belief, memory) is false. Do you now agree that you must rid yourself of this false (habit, belief, memory)?

E. Release the energy in the blockages. This is the most important part of the process of clearing away blockages, as the release of emotional energy makes it possible for the subject to accept the new argument (instructions) that the magician wishes to present to the subject. Until all of the energy in the old patterns are released there will still be a trace of the old patterns to confuse and disturb the subject. If there is sufficient energy left in the old program or patterns, the subject may override the new program or pattern completely.

To rid yourself of this false (belief, habit, memory) you must release all of the emotional energy you hold in that false (belief, habit, memory). You will now release all of the emotional energy held in this false (belief, habit, memory) that keeps you operating your life based upon it.

Take a deep breath, and with the energy of that breath, release all of the emotional energy that you hold in this false (habit, belief, memory).

THE MAGICIAN MUST NOW WAIT FOR THIS BREATH OF RELEASE.

More than one breath of release may be necessary. Each breath of release must be commanded, until a full release of the retained energy is obtained.

F. Locate another blockage, Resolve it and release the energy

in it. This must be done until there are no more blockages to be released!
G. Determine that there are no further blockages to your instructions. The subconscious mind will fail to bring up a relevant blockage to your instructions. The first irrelevant blockage, if any are presented, should be released. Then the subject should be asked if there is any reason why it should not accept the instructions you wish to give it. Usually it will not present a counter argument or a blockage. You are now ready to implant the argument or the instruction you desire.
H. Obtain the agreement of the subconscious mind that the argument (instructions) you are presenting to it are valid.

>'Now that you have rid yourself of all the false habits, beliefs and memories that keep you from acting in accordance with _____, you can agree that this is the way that you wish to act, (behave, believe) in the future. Do you agree that this is correct?'

I. Explain to the subconscious mind just what has to be done to implement the argument (instructions) in their daily life. Go into detail, and be specific about what has to be done by the subject in their daily life.
You agree that you must ___'A'___ in the future. From this time forward, you will ___ 'A' ___ whenever the occasion presents itself to you. You will make opportunities to ___ 'A' ___, especially at ___ 'X' ___ and ___'Z'___.
Whenever___'Y'___ occurs, you will have feelings of ___'B'___. You will think of ___ 'C' ___ and remember to avoid (Not to) ___'D'___.
J. Order the subconscious mind to implement the argument (information) immediately. Exert your will power when you order it to implement the information.

"You agree that this will be your new realm of action. In the future, you will act on this as we have decided. You will have no need to question this decision; indeed, you will feel very comfortable with this decision. You have decided this, and this is the way it will be, from this time forward."

K. Instruct the subconscious mind to put energy into the argument (instructions) that you have given it.

"You desire to implement __'A'__, so now you will put energy into this new belief, (habit, memory or program). This energy will be sufficient to keep it fresh and active in your memory. Over the next twenty four hours you will take pleasure in adding energy to this new habit, (belief, memory or program) until it becomes one of the major habits, (beliefs, memories or programs) of your life."

"Take a deep breath, and with the energy of that breath, vitalize this belief, (habit, memory or program.)"

YOU MUST NOW WAIT FOR THIS BREATH

Over the next twenty-four hours, you will take occasional deep breaths, vitalizing this belief, (habit, memory or program) until it becomes one of the major beliefs, (habits, memories or programs) of your life.

L. Instruct the sub conscious mind, using your will power, that it will now follow the argument you have presented to it from this time forward. Instruct it to completely release any contradictory beliefs, programs, and memories that may now be forgotten.

From this time forward you will operate your life following the belief, (habit, memory or program) which we have decided on. Any contradictory belief, (habit, program, or memory) can be forgotten.

Is there anything that could prevent you from operating your life following the habit, belief, memory, or program we have decided upon?

Wait for the answer; Yes or No. If the answer is YES, you must determine what the subject's objection is and

release the blockages that are present. This must be done until a NO answer is obtained to this question.
M. Remove the memory of the implant of the argument (information) and the work that has been done with the subconscious mind.

"It is unimportant to remember this conversation. You will have no need in the future to remember this conversation. This conversation is unimportant, and you will remember only your decision to carry out these good suggestions leading to the decision we have made, and remember to operate your life based on this new and important information."

N. Dismiss the subconscious mind.

Continue to sleep. Sleep soundly and well. Awaken refreshed to a better life.

FORTH LESSON

Miscellaneous Techniques of Distance Working

I   Visualize the person you desire to influence as if they were seated in a chair before you. Speak with them normally, as if they were physically present. You can be more open in your discussion with them, and you can use arguments that are more forcible with the person if you so desire. Concentrate your influence upon the image of the person you see seated in front of you.

This is a quick technique, and requires neither summoning nor any other regular magical technique. This technique is not as effective as using the full ritual process for making contact with a person, but it may be used in an emergency to force a specific idea into a person. It is most effective when you use it with a person you have worked with previously.

II   Concentrate your mind on the subject and direct a single thought to them. This technique works best with those you have worked with previously. It has its greatest effect when a simple single thought is sent. This technique is very much like the technique of fascination, except that the person need not be present, you need not visualize them, and the thought form need not be as vitalized.

There is often a feeling of rapport that occurs between the magician and the subject when the subject receives the thought. This may occur either when the technique of sending a single thought or another technique of distance working is used. In some cases, this feeling of rapport may become so strong when distance working with a subject that it can cause the development of empathy between them.

III Create a mental picture of what you desire the person to do. Impress this mental picture upon your mentally visualized image of the person using your will power. You must visualize the person doing exactly what you want them to do. It is as if they were an actor, and you were the director in a play. You must see them playing a role the way you wish them to play it. You may use this technique either with the person present or absent, but it is best if you use it with the person absent until you have completely mastered the technique. The mental image must be constructed with care, paying attention to all of the details of the action or behavior that you desire the person to perform.

The application of this visualized image allows and encourages the person to manifest those conditions, and your desires for them, in their daily life. With sufficient force, and repetition, it becomes a script that they will play out in life.

IV Passively tuning into another person, with the magician in a meditative state, will allow the magician to observe the flow of the subjects lower conscious thoughts. The magician may then add or correct thoughts that occur within the mind of the subject. This requires that the magician be very non-reactive to any thoughts that the subject may have. The difficulty is to passively observe the flow of the thoughts, and then interject or correct thoughts as they occur. The introduction of the magician's thoughts into the conscious thought stream of the subject must also be passive and not active. This is one of the best ways to learn another persons thought stream, but it is not easy to use this technique to change a subject's behavior.

OTHER BOOKS BY DRAJA MICKAHARIC

Samuel Weiser of York Beach Maine originally published my previous books. They are now being published by Red Wheel/ Weiser 368 Congress Street. Boston, MA 02210

Spiritual Cleansing—a handbook of psychic protection, first published in 1982

A Century of Spells—a collection of a hundred useful spells, first published in 1988

Practice of Magic—An introductory guide to the art of magic, first published in 1995

These books are all sold on the Internet at Amazon.com

Xlibris is publishing several of my more recent books, They may be reached at 36 Walnut Street, 11th Floor, Philadelphia, PA 19106 Or on the internet at Xlibris.com

Magic Simplified—A series of practical exercises for developing the prospective magician. Published by Xlibris in June 2002

Magical Techniques—A number of useful and lesser known magical processes and techniques. Published by Xlibris in July of 2002

Mental Influence—Information concerning magical techniques of influencing other people without their knowledge To be published by Xlibris in November 2002.

CPSIA information can be obtained at www.ICGtesting.com
Printed in the USA
LVOW050123200313

325091LV00004B/167/A